of related interest

Freaks, Geeks and Asperger Syndrome
A User Guide to Adolescence
Luke Jackson
Foreword by Tony Attwood
ISBN 1 84310 098 3

Asperger Syndrome in Adolescence
Living with the Ups, the Downs and Things in Between
Edited by Liane Holliday Willey
Foreword by Luke Jackson
ISBN 1 84310 742 2

Asperger's Syndrome
A Guide for Parents and Professionals
Tony Attwood
Foreword by Lorna Wing
ISBN 1 85302 577 1

Succeeding in College with Asperger Syndrome
A Student Guide
John Harpur, Maria Lawlor and Michael Fitzgerald
ISBN 1 84310 201 3

An Asperger Dictionary of Everyday Expressions
Ian Stuart-Hamilton
ISBN 1 84310 152 1

ASPERGER SYNDROME, ADOLESCENCE, AND IDENTITY

Looking Beyond the Label

Harvey Molloy and Latika Vasil

Jessica Kingsley Publishers
London and New York

First published in the United Kingdom in 2004
by Jessica Kingsley Publishers Ltd
116 Pentonville Road
London N1 9JB, England
and
29 West 35th Street, 10th fl.
New York, NY 10001-2299, USA

www.jkp.com

Copyright © Harvey Molloy and Latika Vasil 2004

Library of Congress Cataloging in Publication Data
Molloy, Harvey, 1961-
Asperger syndrome, adolescence, and identity : looking beyond the label / Harvey Molloy and Latika Vasil.
    p. cm.
Includes bibliographical references and index.
ISBN 1-84310-126-2 (pbk.)
  1. Asperger's syndrome—Patients—Case studies. 2. Teenagers with mental disabilities—Case studies. 3. Teenagers—Mental health—Case studies. I. Vasil, Latika, 1962- II. Title.
RJ506.A9M65 2004
616.85'88—dc22

                                              2004005034

British Library Cataloguing in Publication Data
A CIP catalogue record for this book is available from the British Library

ISBN 1 84310 126 2

Printed and Bound in Great Britain by
Athenaeum Press, Gateshead, Tyne and Wear

CONTENTS

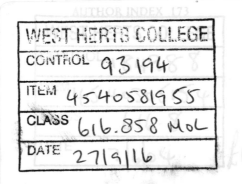

Acknowledgements

The generous contributions of many people helped us to write this book:

First and foremost we would like to thank all the families we interviewed, especially Lee, Rachel, Sarah, Chee Kiong, Luke and Simon, for being a part of this project and for the amazing generosity they showed in sharing their personal stories with us.

Julia Gardner for reading through drafts of the book and offering valuable advice.

Catherine Lee for some great conversations and for commenting on some draft chapters.

The National University of Singapore for providing financial assistance for our research.

Laura Cockburn for all her support and for introducing us to some of the families in this book.

All the autism and Asperger Syndrome organizations in the UK that publicized our project and helped us to locate families in the UK.

Our families for all their support over the years.

Our beautiful and inimitable sons, Rohan and Taran, for being there.

Introduction

Adolescence is a time of transition. The adolescent has one foot still in childhood and one foot tentatively testing the waters of adulthood. It is a time of 'finding one's feet' and defining who we are so that we are able to find our place in the more complex and demanding adult world. In this book we explore how those teenagers whose lives are further complicated by having Asperger Syndrome (AS) grapple with the adolescent quest to find the answer to the question 'Who am I?' Nita Jackson (2002), who recently wrote about her experiences as an adolescent with Asperger's describes this sense of confusion in the process of attempting to define herself as someone with AS:

> I'm confused about the world and its mainstream majority. What would it be like being mainstream? Would I even have these problems if I were a mainstreamer? Is Asperger's syndrome as bad an affliction as I make out? And who am I anyway? Apart from being a representative of my syndrome, who am I, and most importantly, who will I become? (p.49)

How then do teenagers with Asperger Syndrome view themselves and their own lives? To date, most literature on Asperger Syndrome and adolescence falls into three types:

1. accounts of AS as a social learning disorder (e.g. Howlin 2003)

2. effective strategies and tips for managing the AS teen

3. autobiographical accounts.

In this book we take a different approach by conducting in-depth biographical interviews with adolescents diagnosed with Asperger Syndrome to collaboratively create their life stories. Life stories, as distinct from case studies, attempt to provide an inside-out view of people's experiences. We asked the teenagers to talk about their experiences at school, their relationships with friends and peers, their home lives, their interests, and the meaning and impact of the label 'Asperger Syndrome' in shaping their identities and their aspirations. To date, little work has been published that exclusively focuses on the contemporary experiences of teenagers diagnosed as having Asperger Syndrome. As teenagers, they are surrounded by a growing body of literature on AS. They are the first generation to grow up with the label of AS and are part of an emerging AS subculture with its own unique jargon and identity ('Aspie,' 'neuro-typical,' 'mainstreamer,' etc.).

We are also interested in examining the social repercussions of representing adolescents as having Asperger Syndrome. This type of analysis has largely been absent in the literature. We feel it is important to ask whose knowledge and definitions are being represented in the AS literature and whether these representations are reflective of the way the adolescents in this study view themselves. How do individuals diagnosed with Asperger Syndrome feel about themselves, their lives, and the label? Do they feel stigmatized or is it a valuable framework for explaining some of the difficulties they experience in their lives? In other words, how do these adolescents define themselves and do these self-definitions correspond with the 'official' definitions often imposed on them? We hope to address some of these issues in this book. Similarly, it is inevitable that in the delineation of any social group, stereotypes will emerge that shape our common perception of individuals belonging to that group. In our research we hoped to challenge some of these stereotypes about people with AS.

Our perspective on AS is informed by a social constructionist approach to disability (e.g. Oliver 1990) that emphasizes the role society and language play in marginalizing people with physical and neurological or behavioral differences as 'abnormal.' This approach does not deny the existence of impairments and differences, rather it addresses them without attaching value judgments such as 'normality.' This is in contrast to much of the research literature on Asperger Syndrome that largely adopts a medical and deficit approach. Our work focuses on the value of storytelling and personal narratives in the lives of teenagers with AS. How do their own narratives make sense of their lives? What do their stories tell us about the roles parents, schools, and various therapies and interventions play in contributing to the quality of their daily lives? We also explore points of contention between teenagers' stories and the DSM-IV textbook definition of Asperger Syndrome as a chronic pathological condition (APA 1994).

While adult personal accounts of Asperger Syndrome have emerged (e.g. Willey 1999), they are usually written by individuals who have voluntarily adopted the label of Asperger Syndrome as adults based on their own recollections of their 'symptoms' as children. We do not know what effect the *involuntary* labeling of a child as having Asperger Syndrome has on the quality of that child's life. For these children an integral part of their childhood will be learning that they bear the label of Asperger Syndrome and coming to terms with the fact that they are perceived as having a personal pathology or disability.

Our motive for writing this book comes, in part, from our own experiences of Asperger Syndrome. One episode in particular was a turning point for us. Towards the end of a discussion with an experienced therapist working in the area of autism spectrum disorders we were told to put our 'disability lenses' on and imagine that the person with Asperger Syndrome was like someone who has calipers on his legs and that he is as 'handicapped' as anyone 'physically handicapped.' Having Asperger's, she explained, was a constant struggle with this 'monster called autism' that was always 'struggling to get out and rear its ugly head.' It was a compelling and vivid analogy and one that we grappled with intellectually for a long time. From our own experiences we knew for a fact that

Asperger Syndrome posed many challenges and often immense difficulties but was it a disability?

We wondered about the implications of what the therapist had told us that afternoon. What are the implications of trying to reframe your image of a person with Asperger Syndrome so that this person now becomes a victim of a terrible handicap that can, over time and with great effort, be overcome to lead one to the green valley of normalcy? Are individuals with Asperger's disabled? Is this how they view themselves? Or is this a devalued identity placed on them because of rigid social expectations of what constitutes right and normal thinking and behavior? Does the child with calipers on his legs struggle only with the problem of limited mobility or does the disability he suffers lie in society's construction of him as a pitiful victim?

Many clinical accounts of Asperger's, especially those written before the mid-1990s, paint a gloomy and depressing scenario of Aspie life: after a childhood locked in an inner world interrupted only by incidents of bullying, the Aspie faces an adolescence of isolation, culminating in adult depression and failed relationships. These early case studies were often extreme examples, being based on people who had sought psychiatric treatment (e.g. Wing 1981). We were interested in more diverse and detailed *personal* narratives. Where were the stories describing what it was like to have Asperger's that weren't described in the often judgment-ridden language of medical discourse?

We were also concerned about the lack of analysis of what constitutes 'normal.' What is normal and who says so? Are people who are deemed to be outside the boundaries of normality subjected to unfair comparisons with some unrealistic model of exemplary behavior that the rest of us safe within the cocoon of normality are never subjected to? In addressing this very point, Dan Goodley, who has written about the lives of people with learning difficulties, quotes Martin Levine, a person labeled as mentally retarded:

> If someone whispers a lot during the play people might ignore it or get angry. If we whisper it is because we are retarded. It's like we have to be more normal than normal people. (Goodley 2001, p.215)

In other words, are most people's quirks viewed as aspects of their unique and complex personalities, whereas in the case of the person with Asperger's any quirks are likely to be perceived, not as personality traits, but rather as symptoms of their underlying syndrome?

We hope that this book strikes a balance between allowing teenagers to tell their own stories and offering our own reflections on the significance of these stories for our understanding – as parents, professionals and people with AS – of Asperger Syndrome.

CHAPTER 1

Defining Asperger Syndrome

*Hello. I am Martin ... I have an abnormality in my brain
called Asperger's Syndrome, which is a form of autism. No, I'm
not crazy or retarded: My brain functions on a high level, just
differently than yours. My senses work, but the information
they sent [sic] to my brain can get misfiled, or come in on the
wrong pathways. (Can you imagine 'hearing' bright sunlight?)
... This gives me advantages and disadvantages ... I'm not
asking you to feel sorry for me. Because if you pity me, you are
also pitying all the great people like me, for example: Thomas
Edison, Alexander Graham Bell, and Shatoshi Tijjaru (creator
of Pokemon) who all have autistic traits. We're not looking for
a cure for Asperger's; just your understanding, and the
understanding that comes from research. After all, if autism
were cured, society would lose access to many of its great
geniuses and inventors. We need you to accept us and be friends
with us, while we learn to survive and be successful in your
world. ('Martin', http://www.hoagiesgifted.org/
fitting_in.htm)*

Now, more than ever before, there is greater public awareness and
media coverage of Asperger Syndrome. Our most recent internet

search using the key words Asperger Syndrome results in an incredible 128,000 listings. At the time of writing Amazon.com lists 111 books on Asperger Syndrome in its database, published mostly in the 1990s through to the present. Recently a best-selling novel by Mark Haddon, *The Curious Incident of the Dog in the Night-Time* (2003) features as its hero Christopher, a quirky and gifted 15-year-old boy with Asperger Syndrome, although the term never appears in the book. Mark Haddon's novel has sparked interest in Asperger Syndrome, and his portrayal of Christopher has provided a more human face to public perceptions of people with autism; however, it still adds to the mythology of the autistic savant.

A common feature of many of the media reports on AS is the identification, sometimes retroactive, of gifted and famous people that appear to have the characteristics of AS. This has also served to fuel interest in Asperger Syndrome. For example a story on AS in *The Guardian* newspaper entitled 'The high-flying obsessives' says:

> Asperger Syndrome was unheard of 20 years ago. Now it seems to be everywhere. Ludwig Wittgenstein, the philosopher, who designed a sewing machine at the age of 10 and was friendless and teased by his fellow students is thought to have had Asperger's. So too, is long-haired, green-slippered Albert Einstein, who used to lose his train of thought in the middle of giving a lecture. Their modern day equivalent, Bill Gates, the Microsoft chief executive and Windows inventor, has been described as having autistic-type traits: lack of eye contact, poor social skills, a monotonous voice, a prodigious memory and a tendency to rock backwards and forwards during business meetings. (Gold 2000)

Due to its recent emergence there is at present very little definitively known about the causes of Asperger Syndrome or accurate counts of its incidence. Most would agree, however, that there has been a huge surge in the number of cases diagnosed globally. In California, for example, there has been talk of an 'autism epidemic' since the mid-1990s. According to Steven Silberman (2001) of *Wired* magazine, in 1999 California's Department of Developmental Services had twice the number of clients diagnosed as autistic than six years earlier – and that doesn't include those diagnosed as having Asperger Syndrome. In August 1993, 4, 911 children were entered into the Department's database, and by July 2001 this had risen to a staggering 15,441 reported cases. In November 2002 *Time* magazine reported that this figure had risen to 18,000 children. Accounting for this upsurge is difficult at present, given the lack of clear evidence on the causes of AS. Furthermore there is no consensus as to whether the increase is a genuine epidemic or due to an increase in diagnosing cases. Author and clinical psychologist Tony Attwood (2000) suggests that while we cannot definitively know whether the autism epidemic is real or not, it is possible that the huge increase in diagnoses are the result of previously misdiagnosed or undiagnosed cases finally being given the correct label.

What is Asperger Syndrome?

Asperger Syndrome is a relatively new diagnostic classification that, like autism, is defined by three main areas of impairment: in social development, communication, and imagination. As distinct from autism, Asperger Syndrome is characterized by individuals with, at minimum, normal intelligence and normal basic language skills. Uta Frith (1991) described children with AS as having 'a dash of autism.' Lorna Wing (1981) was the first to propose the now widely accepted notion of an autistic continuum or spectrum ranging 'from the most profoundly physically and mentally retarded person, who has social impairment as one item among a multitude of problems, to the most able, highly intelligent person with social impairment in its subtlest form as his only disability...and shading into eccentric normality' (Wing 1981, p.111). The history of autism and Asperger Syndrome, as diagnostic categories, has charted a gradual progression from autism viewed as a severe and uncommon psychiatric condition to the current perspective of a neurological condition that falls along a continuum ranging from severe autism to milder expressions such as Asperger Syndrome.

In 1994 AS was included for the first time in the American Psychiatric Association's *Diagnostic and Statistical Manual of Mental Disorders* (DSM-IV). The full DSM-IV criteria for a diagnosis of AS, using similar terminology to that of the diagnostic criteria for autism, include:

A.   Qualitative impairment in social interaction, as manifested by at least two of the following:

- marked impairments in the use of multiple nonverbal behaviors such as eye-to-eye gaze, facial expression, body postures, and gestures to regulate social interaction
- failure to develop peer relationships appropriate to developmental level
- a lack of spontaneous seeking to share enjoyment, interests, or achievements with other people (e.g., by a lack of showing, bringing, or pointing out objects of interest to other people)
- lack of social or emotional reciprocity.

B.   Restricted repetitive and stereotyped patterns of behavior, interests, and activities, as manifested by at least one of the following:

- encompassing preoccupation with one or more stereotyped and restricted patterns of interest that is abnormal either in intensity or focus
- apparently inflexible adherence to specific, nonfunctional routines or rituals
- stereotyped and repetitive motor mannerisms (e.g., hand or finger flapping or twisting, or complex whole-body movements)
- persistent preoccupation with parts of objects.

C.   The disturbance causes clinically significant impairment in social, occupational, or other important areas of functioning.

D.   There is no clinically significant delay in language (e.g., single words used by age 2 years, communicative phrases used by age 3 years).

E.   There is no clinically significant delay in cognitive development or in the development of age-appropriate self-help skills, adaptive behavior (other than social interaction), and curiosity about the environment in childhood.

F.   Criteria are not met for another specific Pervasive Developmental Disorder or Schizophrenia.

Lorna Wing (Attwood 1998) described the main clinical features of Asperger Syndrome as:

- lack of empathy
- naive, inappropriate, one-sided interaction
- little ability to form and sustain friendships
- pedantic, repetitive speech
- poor nonverbal communication
- intense interest in certain subjects
- clumsy and ill-coordinated movements and odd posture.

It is important to note that within this description of AS there is considerable diversity, ranging from mild to more severe expressions of each of the symptoms described.

Recently some authors have commented on the potentiality for people to move along the autistic continuum during the course of their lives (Attwood 2000; Shore 2001). Stephen Shore writes about his own progression through the autism spectrum likening it to a journey:

> Looking back on my life at age two and a half...I place myself at that time in the moderate range of the autism spectrum. I was mute and had a limited awareness of my environment. Although these traits pointed me towards the severe end of the spectrum, my ability to be engaged via touch and the fact that my mother was able to reach me via imitation moved me towards the middle. My ability to form a close bond with my mother at that time further ensconced me near the midpoint... By primary school, my verbal ability was just about on a par with that of the other children in my class. My special interests in astronomy, weather and other subjects began to appear in first grade when I was eight years old... At this point I was at the lighter end of the spectrum. (Shore 2001, p.147)

Amongst other things, Shore credits his movement through the continuum to positive early intervention by his parents and an excellent teacher during his nursery school years. He also credits maturation of his nervous system and his growing ability with age to reflect on his strengths and weaknesses and hence develop strategies to overcome weaknesses. According to Shore, it was during adolescence that he began to move out of the autism spectrum, although 'residuals' such as difficulties with subtle social understandings remain.

The medical approach to Asperger Syndrome: Diagnosis and labeling

A controversy in the diagnosis of Asperger Syndrome is the accuracy of diagnostic systems such as the DSM. To date, there are no medical tests that identify the presence of AS in an individual, and so a diagnosis is essentially based on the child's behaviors. The subjectivity involved in interpreting people's behaviors and the diagnostic criteria has led to much criticism. In other words, while the DSM-IV definition provides the most commonly used frame of reference for the diagnosis of AS there still remain shades of gray based on variability in interpreting the absence or presence of some features and their severity. Taking as an example the criterion of 'marked impairment in the use of nonverbal behaviors such as eye-to-eye gaze, facial expression, body posture, and gestures to regulate social interaction,' Linda Lotspeich, director of the Stanford Pervasive Developmental Disorders Clinic says: '…the rules of the DSM-IV don't work… How much "eye-to-eye gaze" do you have to have to be normal? How do you define what "marked" is?' (Silberman 2001). Uta Frith (1991) displayed concern over the fuzziness of diagnostic criteria: 'Does it make sense to talk about deficits and exclusive categories? Should one instead talk about normal and abnormal behavior shading into each other? To put it another way, should one look at Asperger Syndrome as a normal personality variant?' (p.23). Two important questions lie at the heart of this debate:

1.   What constitutes normal behavior and where do we place the boundary between normal and abnormal? Similarly, we could also ask whether the range of behaviors considered as

eccentric but normal is becoming smaller as eccentricities, oddities, and quirks become constructed as symptoms of medical disorders.

2. Are expressions of 'abnormality' necessarily always a negative or a deficit?

In contemporary Western societies behavioral and developmental differences are usually viewed as signs of illness; therefore we tend to look to medical science to provide explanations and solutions for them. It is no surprise then that parents of children who are developing 'differently' would seek professional help to provide some sort of authoritative and definitive explanation for their children's often unusual behaviors. The medical view of Asperger Syndrome as a personal pathology is founded on an unquestioning belief in the validity of diagnostic systems such as the DSM. Once a diagnosis has been made, it tends to be viewed as an infallible, scientifically established truth. Some writers have attempted to reframe this view and have criticized the process of diagnosis and the resulting 'medicalization' of learning disabilities. Gillman *et al.* (2000), for example, make the point that 'diagnostic labels, whether they apply to mental, physical or intellectual impairment, are not only descriptive, but also constitutive of peoples' lives. That is, [diagnostic labels] bring forth pathology, create problem saturated identities, and construct careers as patients and cases' (p.403). This is an interesting perspective because it highlights the 'double-edged sword' nature of a diagnosis such as Asperger Syndrome. In other words, labeling people with Asperger Syndrome may help to provide us with an understanding of their behavior but it also brings to the person the full force of medical knowledge and power. The person becomes a 'patient' or a 'case' in need of treatment, therapy, or rehabilitation.

It is important, then, to recognize that the term 'Asperger Syndrome' is something created by medical science – it is a label people have created to explain, understand, and identify neurological and behavioral differences. Furthermore, it would be naive to believe that this label is neutral. As we have said, labels can be double-edged swords bringing with them the possibilities of greater understanding and access to resources and at the same time the potential for social stigma and a devalued identity. A diagnostic label also emphasizes individual pathology at the cost of exploring the role of the social environment in shaping and defining behavior.

Having said this, we do appreciate the real-world value of labels. In fact many people labeled as having AS, and their families, have shared with us that having the label has been the best thing that has happened to them. Often it results in greater self-awareness, better understanding by others and access to resources. We do, however, think it is very important to debate the issues surrounding diagnostic labels. Like Gillman *et al.* (2000) we would argue that a diagnosis such as Asperger Syndrome should be treated essentially as a hypothesis that is neither true nor false. Instead it should be evaluated in terms of its *usefulness* to the person labeled. Does the label open or shut doors? In this way then a diagnosis can be either accepted or rejected by the person receiving it.

Challenging the 'deficit' approach: Is Asperger Syndrome a disability?

An alternative view of Asperger Syndrome that has been gaining ground in recent years is that AS is a neurological difference, or perhaps a cognitive style, as opposed to a medical condition with all its connotations of pathology. Defining Asperger Syndrome as a medical condition involves looking only at its deficits and how the person who has been labeled deviates from 'normal' development. By adopting this perspective, then, we fail to acknowledge any strengths resulting from this different pattern of development or to ask the question: What constitutes 'normal' patterns of development? Within this perspective, treatments are largely rehabilitative, such as social skills training, the goals of which are primarily to 'normalize' the child as much as possible. As Singer (1999a) points out, we often erroneously assume that within every AS child there is an NT (neuro-typical) child waiting to come out. She makes the important point that 'for difference to *be* difference, it has to be given the right to be different.'

Well-known Cambridge University professor of psychology and director of the Autism Research Centre, Simon Baron-Cohen (2000) poses the question: 'Is Asperger Syndrome necessarily a disability?'

Rather than defining AS as a deficiency he argues that it might better be characterized as a *different* cognitive style:

> Using the term 'different' rather than 'deficient' may seem unimportant...but this small shift could mean the difference between whether the diagnosis of autism is received as a family tragedy, akin to being told that the child has some other severe, lifelong illness like diabetes or hemophilia, or whether the diagnosis of autism is received as interesting information, akin to being told that the child is right-handed or left-handed. (Baron-Cohen 2000, pp.489–490)

In exploring the 'deficiency' versus 'difference' argument further Baron-Cohen outlines 12 behavioral features of children with AS that indicate *difference* but do not necessarily imply *disability*:

1.   The child spends more time involved with objects and physical systems than with people.

2.   The child communicates less than other children do.

3.   The child tends to follow his or her own desires and beliefs rather than paying attention to or being easily influenced by others' desires and beliefs.

4.   The child shows relatively little interest in what the social group is doing or being a part of it.

5.   The child has strong, persistent interests.

6.   The child is very accurate at perceiving the details of information.

7.   The child notices and recalls things other people may not.

8.   The child's view of what is relevant and important in a situation may not coincide with others.

9.   The child may be fascinated by patterned material, be it visual (shapes), numeric (dates, timetables), alphanumeric (license plates), or lists (of cars, songs, etc.).

10. The child may be fascinated by systems, whether simple (light switches, spigots), a little more complex (weather fronts), or abstract (mathematics).

11. The child may have a strong drive to collect categories (e.g., bottle-tops, train maps) or categories of information (types of lizard, types of rock, types of fabric, etc.).

12. The child has a strong preference for experiences that are controllable rather than unpredictable.

According to Baron-Cohen the common thread running through these differences is that the child is 'immersed in the world of things rather than people.' In our resolutely social world this immersion in things rather than people is clearly less favored. Taking this perspective then, AS is only a disability because of our cultural biases that give more currency to social adeptness than being skilled with 'things,' and our assumptions that people who are disinterested and unwilling to engage in certain social activities and rituals suffer from a pathological condition. If this expectation was to change, then AS defined as a disability would no longer exist. As we have discussed elsewhere, it is essential to look at the role of society and cultural institutions such as schools in constructing Asperger Syndrome as a medical condition (Molloy and Vasil 2002).

In a recent book, *The Essential Difference*, Simon Baron-Cohen (2003) further speculates that autism may represent an imbalance between two modes of thinking: 'systemizing' and 'empathizing.' Put simply, systemizing involves thinking about and understanding systems or how things work, while empathizing involves thinking about and understanding people. While most people possess both modes of thinking, Baron-Cohen suggests that females are stronger at empathizing while males are more inclined towards systemizing. Autism with its marked characteristic of impaired empathizing, may be an extreme version of the general male profile which favors systemizing over empathizing. This perspective is an interesting one in that it clearly falls in the camp of viewing autism not as a medical disease but rather as a cognitive style. Baron-Cohen argues that if society were more tolerant of people who prefer to systemize and have difficulties empathizing, then life would be easier for people on the autism spectrum.

Researching AS, adolescence, and identity: Collecting the life stories

In this book six teenagers diagnosed with Asperger Syndrome, and their families, collaborated with us in creating their life stories. These stories, unlike case studies that are written from the vantage point of the detached professional, provide us with a non-judgmental and insider view into the personal and social experiences of these teenagers. We feel it is essential that the growing body of literature on Asperger Syndrome include the voices and expertise of those living the experience of having Asperger Syndrome. Narrative research – or the writing up and study of stories – is one means of ensuring that these voices get heard. (For a fuller discussion of the narrative approach to research, see Appendix A.)

In the process of creating the life stories, we interviewed four male and two female teenagers between the ages of 12 and 18. We also spoke with the teenagers' parents. (For a more detailed description of the research process, see Appendix B.) As a group, there were many differences in the circumstances in which they were diagnosed and the ways in which AS affected their schooling, their identity, and their relationships. Each of the teenagers and their families were asked if they would like to use fictitious names to protect their confidentiality. All of the families elected to use pseudonyms except Luke who is already well known in AS circles as the remarkable young author of two books on AS (L. Jackson 2001, 2002).

Three of the six lived in Singapore at the time of the interviews and the other three lived in the United Kingdom. Of the Singapore group, one is a local Singaporean Chinese and the other two are 'expats' (people of various nationalities temporarily living in Singapore and generally thought to be enjoying a relatively privileged lifestyle). At the time we were selecting our interviewees we were concerned that the 'expat' kids might pose a complication in our research in that it would be difficult to tease out the 'Asperger issues' from the other issues facing these teens as 'expats' or Third Culture Kids (TCKs) living in Singapore. TCKs have been described as persons who have spent a significant part of their developmental years outside of the parents' culture. These children then establish relationships to all of the cultures, while not having full ownership in any (Polluck and Van Reken 1999). Being a Third Culture Kid has many implications for the child's school experiences, his or her social relationships and identity. In the end, however, we decided that these teens had interesting stories to tell and would add richness to our knowledge of Asperger Syndrome and identity issues.

The following are thumbnail sketches of the six teenagers we interviewed:

Lee (18): We met Lee just after he had completed his first term at Oxford University where he is studying for a BA in Mathematics and Computer Science. Although Lee achieved very high scores in his A-levels, his previous school history had been marred by many episodes of disruptive behavior, which had resulted in him changing schools in his local area several times. After his difficulties at school resulted in a period of home schooling, his parents sought an evaluation of Lee to try to understand his emotional outbursts at school and difficulties relating to other children. At age 11, Lee was diagnosed with AS and began schooling at a small, specialized autism unit attached to a mainstream school. At this school Lee gradually managed to get back on track academically and in his final sixth-form year was able to be fully mainstreamed. He also started to do regular volunteer work in an after-school program for autistic children. Lee is an outgoing, articulate speaker who shared with us many interesting ideas about AS and schooling.

Rachel (15): Rachel lives in London with her mother and 16-year-old autistic brother. She attends a small specialist school for girls who are deemed vulnerable to bullying or isolation in a mainstream school. As a child she was late to develop speech, favored solitary play, had a range of rigid routines (such as only sitting on red chairs) and had frequent tantrums. She was diagnosed with AS when she was four years old, although she didn't learn that she had AS until she was seven or eight. Rachel enjoys school especially being with her friends. She's somewhat shy with new people, often avoiding eye contact, and is also exceptionally intelligent as proven by her membership of Mensa. Her interests include graphic design, anime comics, pop music, and singing.

Sarah (12): Sarah is the youngest child we interviewed and was only recently diagnosed as having AS, at the age of 11, by an educational psychologist who felt that Sarah's characteristics and her continuing problems at school were not adequately explained by her previous diagnosis of ADHD. Sarah's parents sometimes feel frustrated by the two diagnoses: does she have ADHD, AS, or both? Sarah is very much a 'Third Culture Kid,' who attends a mainstream international school. The family is Australian but they have lived abroad for several years in Holland and now Singapore. We visited Sarah at her home several times and had lengthy, animated conversations with both Sarah and her parents. She and her family were lively storytellers who willingly shared their experiences and many interesting and personal anecdotes with us.

Chee Kiong (17): Chee Kiong is a Singaporean Chinese who was diagnosed at the age of 14 with AS. As a child he had late speech and behavioral problems but was never given an official diagnostic label by the various professionals his parents consulted. Throughout his schooling Chee Kiong has been socially isolated and often bullied. He finds it very difficult to make and sustain friendships and sees this as the major problem in his life. We met Chee Kiong and his mother in their home for the interviews. Chee Kiong was the first teenager we interviewed and our first meeting was probably a bit stilted on both sides, but later interviews became more conversational and relaxed. When we interviewed him Chee Kiong was attending a local junior college and was studying intensively for his A-level examinations. This was a critical year for him academically and he was obviously under a lot of pressure.

Luke (14): Luke is the only teen in this book preferring to use his own name rather than a pseudonym. He lives in Blackpool with his mother, and his three brothers and three sisters. He was diagnosed with AS after his kindergarten suggested that he should be evaluated by the local Autism Research Team following aggressive behavior towards other children. Luke, however, only found out about the AS diagnosis at the age of 12. Luke strongly advocates adhering to a strict gluten-free/casein-free diet, which both he and his brothers, Joseph, who has ADHD, and Ben, who is autistic, follow. At 14, Luke has already published two books on AS: *A User Guide to the GF/CF Diet for Autism, Asperger Syndrome and AD/HD* and *Freaks, Geeks and Asperger Syndrome: A User Guide to Adolescence.* He and his family were also recently the subject of a BBC documentary. Luke was previously bullied at both secondary and primary schools and now attends a local private secondary school where he is still quite socially isolated but no longer bullied. His main interest is computing.

Simon (13): Simon is an Australian-American who strongly identifies himself as American, although he has lived most of his life in Indonesia, Japan, and Singapore. When we interviewed him Simon was attending an international school in Singapore where he had been placed in a small class for children with diverse special educational needs. Simon was unhappy at school and never felt that he belonged in the special class. As an infant, Simon was diagnosed with cerebral palsy and during preschool was diagnosed as 'learning delayed.' A few years later, at around age seven, he was diagnosed with ADD for which he was prescribed Ritalin. When he was 11 his parents suspected that he might have AS. They took him to see a psychologist specializing in autism spectrum disorders who confirmed their view. Simon was keen to be interviewed but often found it hard to express his thoughts and feelings. We met Simon and his family in Singapore shortly before they moved to Indonesia.

Life stories and identity

Obviously, life stories, as narratives, involve more than just simply recounting 'what happened' to a person. Narrative is an integral component of our everyday life. On one level, our experiences as individuals, members of families, or other larger social groups only make sense to us once told as stories. Narrative forms the very basis of our social experience as it is only through shared narratives that we can convey our life experience to other people. We can only understand our own lives as stories and we can only convey who we are and what we have experienced by telling our stories to others.

Finally, it's only through narrative that we can form and present an identity. A valuable distinction can be made between 'self' and 'identity.' The self is the total sum of all our life experiences and how we reflect on those experiences. In a sense, the self is entirely private and encompasses the sum of our experiences and our fears, doubts, aspirations, feelings, and reflections on those experiences. Our self-identity, in contrast, reflects how we choose to present the rather chaotic microcosm of this total sum of experience to another person. The life stories told by the adolescents in this book are not the objective truth but reflect how they see themselves and their experiences at a particular point in time. As they grow and mature they will understand themselves anew and will no doubt tell different stories about their pasts, which with each decade they will see in a different light.

CHAPTER 2

Lee's Story

In terms of self-definition, I wouldn't define myself as an 'Aspie' anymore, but I do see myself as a computer scientist… Look at Bill Gates – he's definitely got Asperger's, and I think that sort of sums up the connection.

Lee is 18 and in his first year of studies towards a BA in Mathematics and Computer Science at Oxford University. Lee lives on campus but is close to his family home in a nearby town. His family comprises his father, who is a civil engineer and a company director, his science teacher mother, younger sister (17), and brothers (13 and 10). He says that he didn't get along with any of his siblings as a child but now feels closer to his brothers. Mathematics and computers are his major hobbies – in his spare time he loves to write computer programs, design websites, and provide friends and family with technical support. We met Lee at his home during his Christmas break after he had finished his first term at Oxford. He spoke very positively about the academic and social aspects of university life. He came across as proud of his academic success, especially in gaining admission to Oxford University, and was very confident and animated when talking about his future career plans. He is bright, articulate, and charming to talk to, although it is easy to imagine that his unabashed confidence could to some people appear as arrogance.

With his exceptional abilities in his academic subjects, his confidence, and his motivation, talking with Lee leaves you in no doubt that he is going to have a very successful career.

Things were not always so good for Lee. Both Lee and his parents told us of his immense difficulties as a child and young teen, and of the roller-coaster ride of mainstream schooling. His mother says that she noticed early on that he was more volatile and aggressive than other children, but because Lee was her first child it was not always easy to recognize how extreme his behaviors were compared to other kids his age. Once their second child was born, when Lee was two, Lee's parents started to become more aware of Lee's differences.

His parents remember Lee as being a late talker – they consulted a speech therapist when Lee was four and a half. The speech therapist suggested that Lee had 'immature speech development' but no therapy was recommended. At the age of five Lee was speaking clearly. At this age Lee started attending nursery school regularly and his difficulties started to become more apparent. His parents remember: 'More often than not when we went to pick him up he would be isolated on a chair in the corner of the room because he had been "naughty."' His parents moved him to a more structured local Convent school, but the behavioral problems and teachers' perceptions of a 'strong-willed and naughty boy' persisted. His parents describe this period:

> He was extremely unhappy at the Convent and he was unable to conform to their rules and would always be cross and upset when he was picked up by us after school. He was always in trouble and after a number of incidents with other pupils he had a whole year when he was not allowed out for breaks. During this time he read almost the entire school library.

After two and a half years his parents changed schools again. At his new school, a local boys' preparatory school, things initially went well: Lee liked his teacher and tried to cooperate to please her. His academic achievement improved. Aggressive incidents with other students, however, continued, particularly in the playground. Lee recalls that often other students would bait him to get a response, but the problem was that while most kids would know to stop when things got to a certain stage he would 'fight to the death.' Things started to fall apart when Lee was placed with a new and fairly inexperienced teacher. His parents said:

> The new teacher had a much more relaxed style of teaching that meant that the lessons tended to be much less structured. This allowed a lot more interaction between pupils leading to more teasing. Lee was unable to cope and his behavior deteriorated and he became more physically and verbally abusive. The relationship with his peers broke down to the extent that they would enjoy winding him up to get the spectacular losses of temper.

Eventually the school felt that they were unable to cope with Lee and he was asked to leave. His parents moved him yet again, this time to another local Catholic primary school. He continued to have problems, and after several aggressive incidents he was permanently excluded from the school. Things got progressively worse for Lee, and his problems continued to escalate seriously as he moved through his schooling. Everyone seemed to be at a loss as to how best to deal with the situation. His parents rightly worried that in spite of his great academic potential his schooling and future would be jeopardized. His parents were always aware of his advanced abilities in areas such as computing: 'Computing had always been a great interest of his, especially programming, and his ability, for example at age 11, was on par with a computing literate graduate.'

After the series of disastrous stints at various primary schools, ending with permanent exclusion from the last, Lee was for several months tutored at home for five hours a week. It was during this difficult time that his parents initiated a statutory assessment of Lee under the 1993 Education Act. It was around the age of 11, while Lee was being schooled at home, that he was diagnosed with Asperger Syndrome. His parents had previously consulted many professionals about his behavioral problems and developmental differences, including a child psychologist, a child psychiatrist, a clinical psychologist, a child neurologist, and a food allergy specialist, but no diagnosis was ever made. Lee and his family speak of the relief at finally having an explanation that made sense to them. Interestingly, both he and his parents describe the diagnosis as a 'key' to getting support. His parents told us:

When we got the diagnosis we were pleased that we could then find the right support for him. We believed it was the right label and incredibly helpful in securing resources. Also it helped immensely when he got into difficulties with people and we could explain to them that he had a problem. Most people were very understanding. It gave us a focus – to find the best support for a bright young lad with AS who was out of school being sort of educated at home by the local authority. It made us feel more sympathetic towards Lee. It certainly relieved us of some of the painful embarrassment we had felt at times.

After Lee was diagnosed he was able to get a place in a Chinnor Resource Unit (a small specialist teaching unit for children diagnosed with autism spectrum disorders that is located within a mainstream school and able to draw upon the school's resources). It was here that things began to turn around for Lee and he was able to get what he describes as the 'best of both worlds' in terms of education. He was able to learn in an environment that was conducive to his learning style, he felt he was understood better, he met other children with Asperger Syndrome but at the same time he was still able to experience the 'real world' by attending some mainstream lessons. Initially he spent most of his time at the unit working primarily one-to-one with his support workers using a very flexible curriculum. He later began to attend some mainstream lessons with a support worker; and eventually in his lower sixth-form year he was able fully to integrate, unsupported, into a mainstream course of four A-levels: Mathematics, Further Mathematics, Chemistry, and Physics. He achieved A grades in all four subjects.

During his time at the Chinnor Resource Unit, Lee began to do volunteer work at the 'Fun Club,' an after school club for autistic children. Here he met and worked with a nine-year-old boy who, like Lee when he was younger, loved to create and invent using old broken electrical equipment. Lee told us how much he liked working with this boy. While both Lee and his parents feel that Asperger Syndrome only very marginally affects his life now, he is still involved in giving public talks about autism and AS, especially his experiences working in the 'Fun Club.'

Lee talks about his life

Schooling: Not jumping through hoops

The first school I recall going to was the Convent. I started in 1989 and I was there for kindergarten, Year 1 and Year 2. I was unhappy there and spent most of my time 'in the corner' for being 'naughty.' The teacher's approach was to 'smack naughty boys,' but confrontation only aggravated the situation and I was often sent to the headmistress. From my perception the main problem was boredom, and that's when the disruptive behavior would come out.

Throughout my schooldays I felt that the teachers were treating me like an idiot, making me jump through hoops. The problem was the rigidity of the system. The message being given was 'There's a syllabus, these textbooks go with that syllabus, you have to do this and this and this before you get to do the interesting stuff.' I just wanted to get straight to the interesting stuff, but I had to go through all their little hoops and in the end it got tedious. I found learning to read and write boring too. Sometimes I would translate on the fly the book I was reading into French just to annoy the teacher and relieve the boredom.

I always loved mathematics, even the boring stuff they subjected me to at school. Luckily my father, who is a civil engineer with a background in mathematics and programming, was able to teach me more advanced mathematics at home. I was multiplying matrices together at the age of seven and computer programming at the age of six. But unfortunately at school they didn't recognize my abilities. At my first school one of the teachers tested me for giftedness. She said she'd seen gifted children before and that I definitely wasn't one. All the teachers saw in me was an extremely naughty boy who refused to do the work, which I kept saying was boring.

The other major issue during this time was my negative interactions with other children. There's always bullying and teasing in the playground. Most kids push and punch, it escalates a little and then they normally stop at a threshold or a breaking point. My problem was that I wouldn't know when to stop. I would continue and could have quite easily beaten someone to death if I hadn't been dragged off. A lot of the aggression at school was retaliation against the kids picking on me. I would attempt to give back as good as I got. I would always have the last punch, as you'd say. The other kids enjoyed getting a reaction out of me, winding me up, like: 'Let's go and spit at Lee he might do something amusing like smash a window' …most likely with one of their heads! My reaction was always totally disproportionate to what they did to me.

After I was asked to leave the Convent I moved to a local boys' preparatory [private] school – lots of testosterone flying about – where my mother worked as a science teacher. My first two years (Years 3 and 4) at this school were good as I had teachers who were able to maintain good discipline in the classroom. These teachers were able to keep order and didn't tolerate people picking on me or me picking on them. Unfortunately in the third year (Year 5) I had a new and very inexperienced teacher and everything started to deteriorate. This teacher wasn't able to control the class, and the bullying and fighting escalated. People would come up and nick my eraser in the middle of the lesson and he wouldn't do anything about it, and a lot of times my reaction would be ten times worse. I might go over and pull their chair away from them or something to that effect. So I would always be the one who got into trouble because what I did was ten times worse than what they did. This teacher was absolutely useless, often even deserting the class. He would disappear for a cigarette break during the lessons, and consequently mayhem would ensue with me versus the rest of the class. Things got a bit violent and there were a number of 'incidents' so eventually I was asked to leave. Because my mum worked at the school it was all very embarrassing and difficult.

After the prep school I went to a crappy little state school in my local area. The classes were very large – about 35 students in a class – and I was generally disruptive. For the majority of the time we had supply (relief) teachers and the quality of teaching was very poor. The children most probably thought 'Oh great – a supply teacher! We can get away with murder.' And most of the time they did! I lasted there one term before I was asked to leave. The remainder of Year 6 I was tutored at home. This worked fairly well because it was one-to-one and at a level and pace suitable to me, but obviously it was untenable as a long-term solution.

It was during this time that I was finally diagnosed with Asperger Syndrome. My parents had to traipse around London seeing various private specialists, and the majority of the medical profession had never heard of Asperger Syndrome at that time. I had no objections to being assessed. I thought hopefully they might actually see there's nothing wrong with me. It's everyone else who's strange. Among other things I also had an IQ test which produced a score of 142. This helped, particularly in terms of various schools' perceptions of me – it sort of shut them up! My reaction at the time of getting the diagnosis was pure relief at finally finding an explanation for my behavior and knowing that here was a key to getting the support that I needed. I saw the diagnosis essentially in terms of the benefits it could provide me, such as access to a good school where everyone could understand me and I could do my best. I never saw it as a 'label' in the negative sense of the word.

After the diagnosis I was able to get a place in a state secondary school about 20 miles away from home that had a Chinnor Resource Unit attached to it. The unit was right on the school campus. It was fairly large, about 10 or 15 of us with Asperger's and maybe 20 with more severe forms of autism. The ratio of staff to students was 1 to 2. When we went to integrated lessons in the main school we would have a support worker with us. Initially I didn't go into any lessons for the first six months. I spent time at the Unit getting to know my support workers who ended up being with me the whole seven years I was there. In fact they even employed someone just to work with me. They accommodated what was best for me at the time rather than worrying about covering the curriculum. For example, during the first six months I could spend a whole day on the computer if I wanted. Gradually I was integrated into the mainstream mathematics lessons, but I was supported by my key worker whose main job was actually to monitor the rest of the class's behavior rather than mine and keep them off my back. At the time the opinions of the kids in the mainstream school never really bothered me. I know some of them looked at us – the kids from the Unit – as freaks but I didn't really have time for them. After their GCSEs I guess they will be able to work in Waitrose [a British supermarket chain]. I did have friends inside the Unit who were around my age and having the same type of extra support. I made good friends with an autistic boy at the Unit who was a few years older than me. He was also into computer programming and designing games, so we got on like a house on fire. We'd spend all day programming together making our own levels in games and writing silly programs. That was a great friendship.

There were problems with the mainstream lessons. Some of the lessons were so disruptive that I didn't attend them. For example, in the science lessons there was acid being chucked around the place. Even though I love science I didn't do any science classes for the whole of Year 8. I didn't feel I would be learning anything as they weren't doing anything too interesting at that stage.

I started science again in Year 9. It was during this time that my love of mathematics also took off. That was when I would use pads and pads of paper just exploring and discovering various topics at home – everything from summations to integrals to rules, a bit of number theory, lambda calculus, and so on. But I was only in the middle stream of mathematics for Year 9 because they didn't think I would do well in the coursework. A lot of the problem was the way in which the coursework is marked. They want you to jump through hoops like showing your working. I'd be thinking 'Why should I show my working? Look I've got the right answer – I did it in one line.' They want to see a page of working. So it wasn't the lack of ability that was the problem, it was the methodology. I remember my Year 9 mathematics teacher told me that she had argued with the Head of Mathematics at the time saying, 'Look Lee should be in the top stream.' He said, 'But look how terribly he did in the coursework.' I think the coursework at the time was discovering Pythagoras' theorem. It was all supposed to be done in a very roundabout way. I basically wrote out in three lines a proof of the theorem which was totally correct and ultimately the objective of the coursework, but of course this wasn't how they marked the coursework. So although I expressed an understanding of the subject, I didn't jump through the hoops I was supposed to. Eventually the work did become more challenging and I did integrate into the mainstream classes without support from the Unit during my lower sixth- and sixth-form years. I completed A-levels in Mathematics, Further Mathematics, Chemistry, and Physics, for which I got all A grades.

Asperger Syndrome and identity

There was a huge build-up of frustration prior to my diagnosis. Throughout my schooling obviously something was terribly wrong but nothing was ever done to deal with the situation. I had to be expelled from three primary schools and tutored at home for several months before anyone would admit to the existence of a problem or that I needed assessing. Even then my parents had to take me to London to be privately assessed. The school and local government authorities didn't do a thing. Plenty of social workers came to see me and just classed me off as a naughty or disruptive boy.

I first heard that I had Asperger Syndrome when I was bugging all the telephone calls for my house. The diagnosis came through to my mother by phone and I just happened to be listening in, being the inquisitive 11-year-old that I was. I had modified an old Walkman so that it was tuned in to the AM frequency that the cordless phone worked on.

After the diagnosis I was able to get the educational support I needed. I got a place at the Chinnor Resource Unit which was attached to a nearby state secondary school and was there for seven years, completing my secondary schooling there. At the Unit I was able to get the best of both worlds — a separate protected environment where my needs were understood and accommodated and at the same time contact with the 'normal' world of regular mainstream school. It was also especially beneficial meeting other kids with autism and Asperger's some of whom shared similar interests to me.

When I was aged 15, one of the therapists at the Unit asked me to come and help out at a 'Friday After School Fun Club' that she ran for autistic children. I did this for about three years. In particular I was asked to work with a nine-year-old boy called James who she recognized as having quite similar traits to me. He reminded me so much of myself at that age. He had been labeled as ADHD but he also had an Asperger trait of a strong interest in technology, computers, and inventing. He loved dismantling old electrical equipment and then creating and inventing working items from the parts. He'd take apart Walkmans and then, for example, tune them into satellites! We'd have no qualms about taking an old TV into the car-park and smashing it up for the parts. When I was younger, like James, I also loved taking things apart and inventing, but then my interests moved on to computer programming. But I still had my old boxes of electrical 'junk' tucked away in the cupboard, and James and I had lots of fun with them. I got along really well with James, and having been through some of the things he was going through I felt really happy to be able to help. I felt he was glad to know someone at the Club who shared his interests of inventing and who was able to relate to him and understand him. Given how rude and disruptive I had been prior to attending the Chinnor Resource Unit, it was extremely gratifying to be able to help people at the Club who were like I once was.

I think Asperger Syndrome only very marginally affects my life now. I don't think it particularly fits or defines me any longer. I've developed my independence. I'm technically living away from home most of the year and I can cope on my own quite easily. I think the change is a combination of being more socially mature – being able to restrain myself and deflect other people's attempts to wind me up – and being able to study something I love. I think that if someone repeatedly annoyed me like they used to do at school my reaction would probably still be disproportionate. But I always relate these things to intelligence. All this petty teasing and bullying is just part of the ethos of some people. These are the people who just don't want to be at school. They're certainly not there to learn. I'm sure you'd very rarely see someone exceptionally intelligent going around bullying autistic children. I noticed the change in my sixth-form year at school. A lot of the bullying that happens during GCSEs just disappears. All of a sudden everyone has a common focus because you don't do sixth-form unless you have a real interest in your subjects. Everyone else just drops out to go work in Waitrose.

In terms of self-definition, I wouldn't define myself as an 'Aspie' anymore, but I do see myself as a computer scientist. I feel there is a clear link between Asperger's and computer science. Look at Bill Gates – he's definitely got Asperger's, and I think that sort of sums up the connection. At present the only Asperger-related issue that exists is that I may do the odd socially inappropriate thing or make an inappropriate comment. Sometimes I feel people misinterpret my actions and comments, particularly some people may interpret my actions as personal attacks against them. Perhaps I don't always conduct things in the appropriate way and don't have a good grasp of all the complex social nuances of society. Often it's just my not knowing the petty social rules, such as: Should I email this person at university and ask them a question or should I go and see them in their office?

A strange misunderstanding happened recently at college. During my first week, the 'Freshers' Week,' there was a lot of drinking going on at various bars. The first night I met a girl in the bar and we all went off to a club. We got a bit close and to cut a long story short it ended up with a sexual harassment complaint against me. She is a law student and claims I was pestering her during the first week. After that first night I saw her again the following week in the same club. She sent one of her friends over to tell me 'Brenda doesn't want to speak to you.' I said, 'Okay, that's fine. I'll leave her alone then.' After that I sent her an email asking what that was all about and the reply was (after a piss-take) 'I'm not interested. Leave me alone and stop pestering me.' I just left it at that thinking 'What a strange girl' and I maintained my distance from her after that. During a drunken evening with a friend six weeks later we went around college with a bottle of spirits offering random friends a drink. At some point we called on Brenda to see her reaction – as expected it was a 'No' and we continued on with our evening. A short while later I invited my grandparents down for a Formal Hall where, as the name implies, you sit and have your meal in the main hall dressed formally in your gown and all the Senior Tutors, the Provost, and the Dean are all at the high tables. Who should we end up sitting with but Brenda and her mother! I think that's what really sparked the whole thing off, because we had been avoiding each other like the plague, and suddenly here we were forced to sit together. I think sitting opposite and seeing me speak to her mother must have really wound her up because the next Monday I was called into the Dean's office. She had proceeded to place a sexual harassment complaint against me through the Dean in charge of disciplinary matters. She told him that she felt intimidated by me and cited the spirit incident. The Dean called me into his office and went through the whole thing. The procedure states he has to try and resolve it informally first. I found it amusing more than anything else, how she could perceive my actions in this way. I believe the matter is now closed. I saw her recently at a student party and when she saw me she made a speedy exit!

Another example of how I'm sometimes affected by 'AS thinking' also happened recently at college. I bought a sandwich using a U-key, which is a card with a solid-state flash chip that you insert in a machine and the money is automatically deducted. I had just topped up the card so

I knew it had £11.25 on it. I put in the card and there was a beep and they said 'it didn't go through.' So I did it again but I could see from the card value that the money had been deducted twice. I told them but they argued that the machine had said 'error' and the money didn't come off the first time. Well I knew for sure it had! I wasn't going to leave it there. I went to the internet and researched the whole system they used. I went back to them with all the diagnostic specifications and error code and showed them exactly what had happened and why. A lot of people wouldn't bother for £1.60 but I knew I was right and they were wrong. After a bit of an argument in the end they just got fed up with me and put back the money.

I think Asperger Syndrome is another perspective on the world. It's certainly helped me with the mathematical side of things. I find it very easy to think in highly abstract terms. I can also solve a Rubik's Cube in two minutes! I don't think of this as a savant skill. A common misconception about people with autism, perpetuated by movies such as *Rain Man* and *Mercury Rising*, is that autists are all brilliant savants cracking government supercodes, and so on. This is not the case. While the IQs of people on the autism spectrum are not Gaussian-distributed (i.e. on a bell-shaped curve) there is a large range of high and low IQs. I think I've had some interesting experiences, and here I am at Oxford now studying mathematics and computer science. However I got there, I did make it in the end. I wouldn't term Asperger Syndrome a disability. One way of looking at Asperger Syndrome versus neuro-typical-ness is that everyone else (NTs) has a gift for emotional or social understanding but they've got this disability in abstract concepts. It all depends on your viewpoint.

Studying at Oxford

I love being at Oxford. To do mathematics at Oxford you've got to be pretty interested in your subject, and that creates a common link amongst people. My obvious passion for mathematics and computer science is one of the reasons I get on so well with my tutors, who are experts in their field. One of my tutors helped to develop a major programming language. I got on really well with him during my selection interview and that probably helped me get admission. One of the reasons I chose

Oxford as opposed to some other university is that I thought that's the kind of place that will accept people like me.

My focus at Oxford is definitely my work, although I do socialize. I certainly wouldn't say I was the most sociable of people and I'm not going to win any popularity contest in my college, but I do have a group of good friends. I don't feel isolated at all. In my college we're split into 'staircases' and I get on really well with this one particular staircase group. We meet just about every night and sample fine wines and generally have a good time.

I get along really well with my tutorial partner, and I'm often over at his house until three in the morning. We're all nocturnal! We sit there and do problem sheets until 3a.m. and then hand them in, and then we'll wake up at 9a.m. for lectures. That's how life goes.

I don't think anyone at Oxford is aware of my Asperger Syndrome label. I don't think it would help in my perception at university to be labeled, though I did put it down in my application forms to various universities. It helps to fill in their disability quotas. I also thought that if I did happen to run into any difficulties at university at least I'd have some sort of valid explanation. I could pull out the application card and go, 'Well actually how can you expect me to understand what this is all about?' But really in terms of the academic stuff, or even the social stuff, I don't need the label at all. I think it would just complicate matters, especially in the forming of social relationships, if I went around telling people.

Friends and girlfriends

During childhood I had one close friend. It started as an arranged friendship. My mother knew someone through the church who had a son starting at the Convent school at the same time as me. So I went by his house and we played Lego and got to know each other. We started the Convent together knowing each other. And then we both ended up having the same unhappy experiences there and so we moved to the Prep school. I left there after three years but he remained for an extra year, and all the bullying that I had been receiving there was turned on him. He had a really miserable time and eventually left. He's now at university studying philosophy. We're not at the same university but we still keep in touch and see each other. We've been best friends the whole time.

In general I feel that girlfriends at university are a waste of time. You're at university to study and I think it's a huge distraction. I'm sure the people with girlfriends don't do all their work. I've had two girl-friends – two internet girlfriends. My first girlfriend was Marie who is French-Canadian and lived in Montreal. We used to talk every night via a net meeting. Obviously it wasn't a physical relationship and we didn't go out, but it was emotional. We saw each other via webcam and we formed quite a close relationship. We even planned to meet each other during the summer holidays in the Caribbean, where my aunt and uncle own a rental business. Unfortunately, her dad became quite sick and she couldn't make the trip. So I went off to this Caribbean island for eight weeks where the internet is scarce. We didn't talk for about eight weeks and during that break she got up to no good.

When I came back and talked to her online she was suddenly very distant. She told me that she'd accidentally met this guy, 'just a friend,' and gave me enough information about him that I was able to hack into his computer where I discovered some rather incriminating photos of him and her together as well as his CV. His CV had his number on it so I rang him up and she answered the phone! So that was the end of that.

My future plans

I see myself as completing a degree and possibly a couple of postgraduate degrees in computer science or computer science-related fields. On an intellectual level, I'm very interested in exploring artificial intelligence as a research topic, but employment-wise I'm likely to work as a program-mer for a software company such as Microsoft after completing my studies. I'm already a founding member of a computer company that I recently started with some friends. We're doing some good jobs at the moment during the holidays – we've already finished a ticketing database for club tickets so people can buy tickets using the web and mobile phones (WAP/SMS). I'm interested in moving to another country to work for a few years, possibly Australia or somewhere in Europe.

CHAPTER 3

Rachel's Story

One of the reasons I joined Mensa was that I wanted to use it as a hallmark of my intelligence and say 'I have this amount of intelligence and can prove it because I'm in Mensa!' On the whole I do think most people with Asperger's tend to be fairly intelligent. If I could change myself and get rid of the Asperger's, I honestly don't think I would because I'm sure I'd lose part of my intelligence.

Rachel is 15 years old and lives in the Greater London area with her mother Helen and 16-year old brother James, who is autistic. Rachel's parents separated when she was four but Rachel's father lives close by and she stays with him every third weekend. Rachel has never attended a mainstream school and is currently a day pupil at a small residential specialist secondary school for girls. When Rachel was seven she received a statement of educational needs that outlined several key needs based on a general assessment that Rachel had 'complex social, emotional and communication difficulties.' Rachel's mother Helen has always advocated that Rachel attend specialist schools rather than mainstream. Rachel's current school is for girls who would be emotionally or physically vulnerable in a mainstream setting. Students at this small school (it has a maximum enrolment of 56) include those with physical disabilities, learning difficulties, and those who are performing well below their potential. Rachel is in a Year 10 class of only six students. She also attends French and history classes in a nearby large mainstream secondary school. Helen is very positive about the benefits of specialist schooling and particularly praises Rachel's current school:

> Her school is for girls of average and above intelligence but who would be vulnerable in a mainstream school. So there are some Aspies there. Her best friend is there because she has facial disfigurement. So they're all very accepting of people as people rather than as syndromes. It's actually a delicious, delightful school – just wonderful. It's like an Enid Blyton book. It's a big Victorian building with acres of grounds.

Helen says the only problem she can see in relationship to specialist schooling is distance as often the schools are not local. Rachel's school is an hour's drive away, which means all her friends are also at a distance making regular after-school and weekend contact difficult.

Rachel was diagnosed with Asperger Syndrome at the age of four. Rachel's older brother had been diagnosed with autism earlier, so the family was very aware of issues relating to the autism spectrum. To begin with Helen had no concerns about Rachel's development but then gradually she noticed some emerging language and social difficulties:

> Initially I just thought what a good kid. She plays so nicely and her play was always constructive. It wasn't piling things up or lining things up. She was very creative in her play. And unlike her brother she could occupy herself beautifully. But she didn't have language. And she didn't like being with other children. She just could not bear children approaching her. If they touched her it was like World War Three. She hated noise and she hated nursery when they had singing or music. And there was rigidity like she'd only sit in a red chair. She was also showing signs of extreme perfectionism. She was very hard on herself and if she couldn't do something she would scream and have a tantrum.

Rachel found out she had Asperger's when she was seven or eight. A friend of Rachel's at the time had Asperger's and was very open about being an Aspie. Rachel also came to identify herself as an Aspie by recognizing the many similarities between herself and her friend. Although Helen had always openly talked about autistic spectrum disorder (ASD) issues at home, it was only at that stage that Rachel actually realized that she had Asperger's. Helen feels that in no way has the label had any negative repercussions for Rachel, such as discrimination or stigma. In fact Helen says that from her perspective as a parent the label has been only positive in terms of helping to secure the right support and services for Rachel:

> I don't think the label has affected Rachel in any way. She did a magazine interview which is about teenagers and Asperger's. It was a normal girls' magazine and they wanted people to have an insight into autism. In the article Rachel said it's not really part of my life. I'm me rather than an Asperger person. For me it was important because it meant I could demand facilities that were required. There was a label that I could hang her needs on and say you must address these needs because she has Asperger Syndrome. So to me, even though there's a lot of controversy about labeling, there's a lot to be said for it as long as the facilities are there and you can access them.

Both Rachel and Helen now see the Asperger's as almost incidental to Rachel's life as a teenage girl. Helen says:

> I think a lot of Rachel's concerns now are around being female and adolescent rather than being an Aspie. I don't think the biggest problems in Rachel's life are those resulting from having Asperger's. I don't think she feels it holds her back at all.

Helen did say, however, that one significant issue remaining is that of Rachel's difficulties with crossing roads and traveling independently. In fact she has almost been run over a couple of times:

> She can walk her route between school and the mainstream school where she goes for some classes because she was supported for about a year and they walked her back and forth and she manages that now all independently. That's fine – she's got her specific route. But she's still not great in crossing roads, particularly here on the main T junction. She's not confident or

competent in her road safety skills. Something I am planning on doing is start taking her on bus routes so ultimately she is able to do that independently. But her travel skills are definitely not those of your average 15-year-old.

At one time Rachel closely identified with Asperger's and autism, seeing herself as an Aspie rather than as 'Rachel.' Helen feels that it was Rachel's play/art therapy that eventually helped her to see herself as a unique and valid person and not an embodiment of Asperger Syndrome:

> When Rachel was about ten years old her play/art therapist noted that she was overly identified with being autistic and having Asperger's and not seeing herself as a person, and a lot of what happened in the play/art therapy helped her to see that lots of the stuff she did and felt and thought was actually a function of being her rather than being an Aspie. She was given a space where she could explore the idea that she is simply Rachel and not Rachel the Aspie. For example, the therapist had said to her, 'You can have strong likes and dislikes about people without being autistic or having Asperger's.' And apparently Rachel just burst into tears and said, 'Oh I didn't realize that happened to normal people too.'

At the time Rachel felt an aversion towards people with special needs. Her brother James attended a respite care place for children with very special needs and multiple handicaps; Rachel experienced strong feelings of repulsion and fear when she went there but didn't realize that other people had these sorts of reactions too. Rachel's feelings about autism and Asperger's as a child were clearly colored by having an autistic older brother. Helen says that having an autistic brother probably made Rachel fearful of autism and Asperger's:

> I suspect that while Rachel may not have been overtly aware of it she probably had this fear because of her brother that, 'Oh my god is this what being on the autistic spectrum means?' There was also the bit that she was aware of, which is that this is a pain in the butt. This child is making this family damn disruptive and dysfunctional. She would get angry that she had tantrums and that a lot of the kids that she had difficulty with at school had

similar personality traits to James. So for her it was, 'God there's no escape! I get my brain done in at home by James and I go to school and there are another set of Jameses there.'

One of Rachel's defining characteristics is her intelligence. She joined Mensa when she was about 11. Helen is also a member of Mensa and describes how Rachel came to join:

> Rachel started to play the online kids' Mensa games and she just adored them. She played with them morning, noon, and night and did absolutely brilliantly at them. So we applied for a test pack and she did that and did really well. Her IQ was 152 the last time it was measured.

The motivation to join Mensa was to have Rachel's intelligence recognized. Helen says:

> I thought it would be really valuable because her primary school had been brilliant. When she first went in there she was a screaming wretch, and through all that they recognized the academic ability in her. I wanted to make sure that no other school or academic placement was going to be unable to recognize that. We could always say, 'Yes she has difficulties but she is a member of Mensa so don't labor under the misapprehension that she is not bright!'

Rachel has a wide range of interests but none of her interests could be deemed obsessive. Rather she tends to be passionate in her hobbies and interests. Like many teenagers Rachel loves music – indie, rock, grunge, and nu-metal music. She has a strong interest in Japan and all things Japanese that originated with her interest in manga and anime comics and Japanese video games. She is strikingly talented in creative writing and drawing. She loves ICT – web surfing and chatrooms – and one of her many possible career choices is to be a website designer.

Rachel wears dark-rimmed glasses and has dark shoulder-length hair. For our first interview, on a Tuesday evening, she was dressed casually in her school uniform jersey and comfortable pants. She did not strike me as the type of teenager who has to be dressed in the latest fashionable brands and is more inclined to have an individual style and taste in clothes. Her mum supports this view by mentioning that Rachel was very much an 'anorak' but that she's recently started to take an interest in shopping.

We sat at the lounge table and as soon as we began the interview I noticed that Rachel avoided my gaze. Throughout the entire interview she kept her eyes on her fingers and picked and fidgeted at a cane fruit bowl on the table. Only at the very end of the interview did she open up and begin talking about the problem of eye contact. By the end of the second interview, Rachel was a lot more comfortable and outgoing and I noticed that we were engaging in a lot more direct eye contact with each other.

Rachel's voice can seem unusual at times. She told me that she's often teased about having 'a posh accent.' Often she can become quite loud, almost booming. At the same time, Rachel is highly entertaining, expressive, and eloquent. She shows a great deal of passion and enthusiasm in her speech and displays emotion when discussing painful events. She also has a fantastic reading voice and can read entire passages of prose flawlessly. Rachel and Helen appear to be extremely close, and throughout the interviews there seemed to be an almost unspoken rapport between them – as well as much playful teasing of each other. As well as being mother and daughter they are clearly good friends.

Rachel talks about her life

Asperger Syndrome and identity

I would describe myself as noisy, weird, individual, loyal, passionate, and a mummy's girl! Like most teenage girls I sometimes worry about my appearance – for example, is my nose too big, or my eyebrows too hairy, or my face too square, or am I too fat? But on the whole I'm fairly happy with myself. If I could change myself into anyone I'd like to be Kelly Osbourne from my favorite show *The Osbournes*. I think she looks quite cool and she gets on really well with both her mum and dad.

The things I most enjoy doing are listening to music, surfing the net, playing video games, and studying Japanese. I also like drawing cartoons, especially anime characters. When I was younger I used to make up my own cartoon characters. From about the age of 9 through to 14 I had created literally hundreds of characters and all the characters had their individual personalities. What really perks me up is belting out a great tune. 'She's in Fashion' by Suede is a really good song to get me going. What stresses me out the most is my brother babbling, which he does when he's on the PlayStation sometimes. I tell him to shut up or I'll groan to try and get the message across, but it usually doesn't. He also likes to tell little stories to himself and he even does the different voices for the characters.

I sometimes see myself as 15 going on two because I can be really silly and immature. At school I'm one of the noisiest girls in my whole class. I wouldn't call myself disruptive but perhaps disruptively noisy. I was talking to my best friend on the internet the other night and she said sometimes the teaching assistants look at me as if to say 'Oh my god she is just so silly.' Although I know I'm being silly, and I shouldn't be doing it because it annoys other people, I just do it anyway out of boredom. I'm usually just trying to lighten the lessons up a bit by being silly. I can also be annoying at home. Usually I'm really tired after school but I get a second wind after I've had my shower at about 6.30 and then if Mum's on the computer and I want to use it, or if I'm simply bored, then I'll deliberately annoy her.

I first found out I had Asperger Syndrome when I was about seven or eight. I remember going around the playground and telling the other kids 'I've got Asperger Syndrome' as if I was quite proud of it in a bizarre way. The kids were 'Mm yeah whatever' like totally disinterested in it. At my school there are other kids with Asperger's so I don't really get teased about it. When I was younger I think I was probably frightened by Asperger's and autism. I remember when James used to have really bad phases I would say to Mum that he should be put away in a Warden's Home. There were times when I literally just hated him because he was behaving so badly. I also really hated people with certain special needs and found them quite scary. James, when he was younger, went to a place for children with very special needs and lots of them were multiply handicapped. I would just freak out when we went there to drop him off or pick him up. I was completely scared. I feel less scared now because I realize that I'm not the only one that feels that way and that it's a normal reaction. Now I can see people who rock or flail about and hit themselves and on the whole I'm cool about it. Once when I was rehearsing for a Christmas choir service at another school, there was a girl nearby who was on the floor crying and yelling her head off. My friend was like, 'What's the matter with her? Do you think she has epilepsy?' and I'm like, 'Oh don't worry – I'm used to that sort of thing!'

About a year ago I was featured in an article for a regular girls' magazine about different teenagers' insights into living with autism. In the article I said I don't feel that Asperger's holds me back and I think that still sums up the way I feel at present. I don't think I have as many obvious features of Asperger's as I did when I was little. I think I have learnt to overcome most of the social interaction problems that are supposed to be a feature of Asperger Syndrome. I don't feel I have problems with empathy or understanding what other people are thinking or why they do certain things. Sometimes I will say something bizarre, but that's actually quite rare and it's difficult for me to describe some of these bizarre things because they *are* so weird but on the whole I don't have problems with language, such as understanding idioms and so on. In the past one of my problems was that I would say things like 'Look at that fat lady!' and exactly what I was thinking, but I've learnt over time to 'think but not say.' Mum says I'm now very sensitive socially.

I don't really have problems 'reading' social situations but I can still be quite gullible. For example, one of my classmates was talking to me on the internet one night and she told me she'd done it and was pregnant. She's not the sort of girl I would have ever expected to even go out with a boyfriend. Anyway I fell for the story and I was actually crying because I was so upset about it. Later her boyfriend rang me and said I was a 'muppet' for falling for it. But I wasn't offended because I can be pretty gullible and I'm not always sure when a person is joking or being serious.

I can be quite shy around new people. And sometimes if a person is in trouble I deliberately stop talking to them because I'm worried about upsetting them by asking 'What's the matter?' A couple of years ago one of my aunts died and I used to get really upset about her. My mum was upset too, only I'd try and put on a brave face in front of Mum and bottle it all up because I didn't want to upset her even more.

One of the problems I still have in social interaction is making eye contact. I'm not exactly sure why I have difficulty maintaining eye contact but I think the sensation of being stared at by the other person causes the problem. I remember a couple of years ago during a lesson on life skills at school we were role-playing how to welcome someone in and offer them coffee and so on. The teacher shook my hand but I didn't look at her so she asked me to try the role-play again, but this time with eye contact. I still wasn't able to look at her the second time, and when we tried again the third time, I did look at her and then just burst into tears. I think a lot of it depends on my emotional state, and I don't really have control over it even when I know my eye contact must appear very askew. I've tried looking at the forehead instead of the eyes and that helps sometimes, but when I'm feeling really uncomfortable I don't want to look at the face at all. Most of my friends at school don't mind that I don't always make eye contact with them because they are used to it.

A feature of Asperger's I do identify with is obsessions. I don't have any strong ones at present but I have to admit I am pretty obsessed about the band Gorillaz, but it's not so bad that I eat, sleep, and dream them, although I have had one or two dreams about them. I can carry on with my life and it's not as if they totally rule me. One of my previous obsessions was with a video game character called Crash Bandicoot. When I first saw him I just thought he was so cute that I totally fell in love with him for about three or four years. I didn't actually stop obsessing about him until last year. While the obsession wasn't so bad that it completely took over my life, if someone said 'Crash Bandicoot' I'd be like, 'What about him?! What about him?!' and get really excited. I'm also addicted to pencil cases. My obsession with pencil cases started fairly recently. Whenever I'm out shopping I'm like, 'Oh, that's cute – I have to get that!' I really love stationery and if I see a cute piece of stationery I just have to buy it. My other big interest, Japan, oddly enough started with a music video by the Vengaboys. It was filmed in Tokyo and I was like, 'Wow, it just looks so incredible!' But the interest could also be partly due to the fact that I was really into video games and most video games come from Japan.

My mum says one of the biggest signs that I'm Aspie is my obsession with collecting magazines like *Top of the Pops* and then cutting them up before recycling them. I can never just recycle a whole magazine. I just have to go through it and then I'll spot something my friend might be interested in and I'll cut it out. I'll go on cutting out all these pictures until I'm left with these tiny shreds of paper. Sometimes I'll be up until three in the morning cutting out the magazines to recycle and then I'm so tired. Mum will say, 'You don't need to cut them out to recycle them. You can just give them to me.' But I guess I just have this need to do it. Often I get to school and my friends don't even want all the pictures I've cut out for them the night before!

If I had to describe the positive aspects of Asperger Syndrome I would say intelligence. While this may not necessarily be true for every person with Asperger Syndrome, for me part of the outcome of Asperger's has been my intelligence. One of the reasons I joined Mensa was that I wanted to use it as a hallmark of my intelligence and say 'I have this amount of intelligence and I can prove it because I'm in Mensa!' On the whole I do think most people with Asperger's tend to be fairly intelligent. If I could change myself and get rid of the Asperger's, I honestly don't think I would because I'm sure I'd lose part of my intelligence.

Asperger Syndrome and socializing: Enjoying my friends

I think a good friend is someone who is loyal and doesn't talk about you behind your back. It is someone who is understanding and a shoulder to cry on. A good friend is someone who is fun and a nice person and with whom you share some things in common, but not necessarily everything. When it comes to making friends I don't really have a problem and on the whole I find it is other people who make friends with me. My best friend at school, Alex, has something called Cruzon Syndrome which is where the facial bones grow abnormally. When I was younger I used to really hate other people with special needs but as soon as I saw this Cruzon girl I thought she seemed really cool. There was just something about her that I really liked.

My friends know I have Asperger's and one of my friends has got it too. Before she came into my class in Year 10 she visited the school for a few days and we got along really well. One day when we were out on a school trip I was just chatting to her and she asked me what special needs I had. I told her I had Asperger's and she said, 'Oh me too!' We're both quite artistic and we both like making things.

One of my good friends is the niece of the speech therapist at my old school. When I was in Year 6 I was asked by the speech therapist to draw pictures showing different emotions. She then asked me if I'd mind if she took the pictures home to show her niece. I said that was fine. Her niece then wrote back to me and asked if we could be pen-pals and we've been friends ever since. We see each other about every half term and go to the theater or shopping or eat at a restaurant.

I don't really see my friends much at the weekends because of my brother. Although he's not around much these days, when he was around, having friends over was definitely a problem because he finds socializing extremely difficult. Often he'd behave in a fairly typical autistic way – talking to himself, bouncing around, babbling and talking about some pretty strange stuff – and my friends got a little freaked out by that. Not that they'd say, 'Ooh he's autistic, what a freak.' But they would probably think, 'What is going on here?'

I'm not really interested in having a boyfriend. Not many of my friends are really that boy mad or have boyfriends either. Sometimes I do think about it but not very often. I wonder how I can be friends with a boy before he becomes my boyfriend because I read somewhere that all the best relationships start out as friendships. But I guess I find it easier being friends with girls than boys at the moment. I have to admit that I do have quite a lot of crushes on guys and when I go down to the mainstream school for lessons I do see the occasional guy there and think, 'Hmm he's cute.' And once there was this seriously cute guy there who I see quite a lot and he wore a chain on his school trousers and I thought, 'Mmm I'd really like to give that chain a good tug.' But I didn't!

Bad tempers and the blues

If there was one thing I could change about myself it would be my temper. Being teased has never been a problem for me, and in all honesty it's more often me that's being the bully. When I was in primary school there were these kids that I decided that I didn't like and I was quite horrible to them. Most of the kids I bullied were just ordinary innocent kids who weren't really sure how to make friends and were annoying purely because of that. I used to deliberately leave this one girl out of things just to be mean, and there was this other girl I didn't get along with and I used to steal her glasses. But I think it's more recently that my bad temper has come out, and although I'm not normally a violent person if someone cheeses me off I am more likely to hit them. I'm almost never angry at home. It's mainly when I'm at Dad's or at school that I get cheesed off and where I find getting on with people slightly more difficult. When it's just me and Mum we get on perfectly fine. But sometimes when my brother's being particularly annoying or my dad's doing something that I'm not really happy about I actually swear at them.

There is one girl in my class, Jenny, who I find extremely annoying. She just never leaves people alone and she's always touching you and generally just invading your space. She's very silly and immature and she just gets on my nerves. In fact we aren't allowed to sit next to each other any longer at school after what happened recently. I was in the school toilets and both Anna, my friend who also has Asperger's, and Jenny came in. Jenny was giggling and holding Anna's pencil cases, which she had taken. Anna is one of my friends so I just got really angry that Jenny had taken something of hers. I yelled loudly 'Give them back!' and then I thumped Jenny quite hard. I got detention for a whole week. At the time I felt that the school's reaction was really over the top because I didn't really see how defending a friend is so wrong. I was very upset that my mum and the head teacher were so disappointed in me. The head teacher actually called it an assault, which I still think is a little stupid, but I do see now that it was wrong for me to do what I did.

I have phases where I feel depressed for ages and ages. I think I especially experience these phases when I have problems that I bottle up. When I first started to get these phases I'd have them literally for a couple of months. Then eventually I'd go and talk to Mum about it and I'd feel a little bit better than before. I also find that if I listen to Linkin Park too much and some songs in particular I remember my dead aunt who I was very close to and I just get really upset. I've never had to take medication for depression but I am concerned that I might have to one day.

When I'm really upset I only like to talk about it with Mum or my best friend Alex. They're the only ones who can cheer me up out of it. If something's bothering me at school I'll usually wait until I get home so that I can talk about it with Mum. We usually brainstorm strategies for handling difficulties. But often the problem has already got out of hand by the time I get home. I do find it difficult asking for help. When I'm really upset or angry I usually just sit around and go really quiet or maybe cry. Sometimes I'll listen to some really sad music. Once when I was in a maths lesson the teacher was really p——-ing me off and I got so angry that I bit myself. I don't bite or scratch myself as often as I used to – only when I'm really, really angry. When I was about ten years old there was an incident at school where I got terribly upset because the teachers were forcing me to play with the kids at playtime and I hurt myself really badly. The teeth marks were there for weeks afterwards.

My family

I don't really hate my brother but I don't really love him either. We just tend to stay apart and do our own thing. I would describe the relationship as fairly distant. We don't share common interests – he's into films and classical music whereas I'm more into modern music and art and video games. He acts on these mad whims. For example once he just picked up my mum's address book and started randomly ringing up people from the book at about nine o'clock in the morning. I must say he was very popular for doing that! I'm being sarcastic about that of course!

I was about four when my parents separated. When I go around to other friends' houses, like my best friend Alex, and see her mum and dad all happy together, I think what I wouldn't give to have a mum and dad like that and it makes me really sad. I stay with my dad every third weekend, Friday evening until Sunday evening. I wouldn't describe our relationship as particularly good. He has cable TV and I like nothing better than to sit in front of the box and watch the music channel with the volume up fairly loud. But Dad either complains that the song is awful and yells at me to turn it down or if it's Kylie Minogue, or practically every other girl in Pop, he drools over them and I feel like saying, 'Oh god why do you do that?!' Dad doesn't really like me to just blob out in front of the television. Actually, he puts pressure on me sometimes. I remember once he saw some of my drawings – mainly of cartoon characters – and he just went over the top saying stuff like, 'Oh, you must sell these over the internet!' With Dad, there's always this pressure there to do well. Although I find it really hard to get along with my dad he can be quite sweet sometimes. The last weekend I stayed with him he kept asking me whether I'd like to do some painting, and I kept saying 'no thanks' because I was doing my homework. I felt so upset because he wanted me to paint but I wouldn't do it. He was being sweet to me yet I just felt so angry and pressurized.

My future plans

I see myself going to college to learn Japanese, art, IT, and languages, probably at the university near here which has a special needs unit. I'm still unsure about university but if I do go then it will definitely be nearby so I can still live at home with Mum. I'd like to work in either the arts or media. I can see myself as a graphic designer, or working in some form of computer-aided design, or perhaps as an illustrator or copywriter. Mind you, I'm also very keen on Japanese, so who knows?

CHAPTER 4

Sarah's Story

When I was younger I would make my own animals in my imagination. I'd have a big imaginary eagle called Corix and he'd sit on my shoulder. Once I was climbing a big rock with my mother and when we got to the top it was there, my imaginary horse. It was so real, so solid.

Sarah is a 12-year-old Australian girl living in Singapore with her parents and nine-year-old brother. When Sarah was seven the family moved from Australia to Holland, where they lived for four years before moving to Singapore. Last year Sarah was diagnosed with Asperger Syndrome by a psychologist in Singapore. Up until then Sarah had been variously diagnosed as having speech and language disorders, dyspraxia, and ADHD.

Initially, delays in Sarah's language development prompted her parents to seek professional advice. When she was three, her parents were concerned about her tendency to speak in short unintelligible sentences, her poor articulation, and her short attention span. She was assessed by a speech language pathologist as having a developmental language disorder and received speech therapy for several years. Her mother, Catherine, recalls Sarah's hyperactivity at this time:

> She played very sporadically. It was a very small attention span. She never drew, never would sit down and do anything where you had to sit down. Even when she was at preschool they had to stand her up to draw because she was always moving. She loved playing with children but she'd always end up getting over-excited and biting them.

As she grew older, Sarah continued to display hyperactive behavior, inattentiveness, and learning problems. When she was eight, Sarah was diagnosed as having ADHD and was prescribed Ritalin, which she continued to take until recently. Sarah's parents believe that the Ritalin initially had a huge positive impact on her ability to focus and perform well academically at school. But eventually, the effects began to plateau. Catherine recently consulted a psychiatrist, who suggested that Sarah's Ritalin dosage had not been increased in proportion to her growth and was therefore having reduced effects. Recently, Sarah's parents decided to stop the Ritalin because of concerns about the side-effects from long-term use, although they were still in two minds as to whether they should re-introduce it at a later time.

Sarah was recently told by her parents that she had Asperger Syndrome and responded positively to the news. She felt the label described many of her characteristics and finally provided an explanation for why some aspects of her life were challenging. AS gave her a reason for why she was different. Catherine describes Sarah's positive feelings about AS:

> I think because she got the diagnosis at the same time she joined the AS social skills group she thought she was a part of something and it made her feel special. Now she's trying to tell me that she thinks her best friend at school has it and she should come and join the group too! I think she sees it as something that makes her special. We framed it in a positive light and she thinks it's pretty groovy because Bill Gates has got it! But I don't think she really understands it that well. She's just taken what she wants to understand of it and has picked out the bits she wants to hear.

For Sarah's parents, the latest diagnosis of Asperger Syndrome has been confusing and often difficult to reconcile with Sarah's previous diagnosis of ADHD, especially as two of the professionals that they regularly consult have differing opinions as to whether Sarah has AS or is showing behaviors characterized by unmanaged ADHD. Catherine, speaks of the conflicting diagnoses:

> I've got two different people telling me two different things. I mean, what framework do you look at? When Sarah throws a wobbly – a tantrum – and we ask, 'Is Sarah throwing a wobbly because she is tired and overactive or hyperactive from school – the ADHD viewpoint – or is she throwing a wobbly because she cannot perceive what's going on and she's misunderstood a social cue?' Now, how I deal with a tantrum depends on which way I look at it. Do I deal with it by calming her down or do I deal with it by reasoning with her, by trying to explain? That's our dilemma. To give you an example, Sarah had an explosive behavior recently, the worst in months, just two days after school started back. Was it because of the change of routine, a transitioning thing, or was it because she was confused? What happened is she came down with her school clothes and they were the wrong ones. I went 'Oh' and smiled at her. As soon as I did it I knew I had done the wrong thing. My smile was like 'Oh you poor thing, you've done all this work and you've got it wrong and you'll have to do it all again,' and she thought I was laughing at her. And then she exploded. I think she has got both AS and ADHD but it's very hard to pull apart what is causing what problems like her explosive behavior.

Sarah's father, Peter, is not so sure that Sarah has both conditions:

> I think she's got ADHD but I'm not as convinced about Asperger's and I do view Asperger's as the latest train to come into the station so everyone is getting on board. But I'm happy to go along with it because of the Asperger group she's going to and the social skills she's picking up from the group and the way she comes out feeling from it seems to be making a difference.

> There are two major things I see about Asperger's: firstly, there is the obsessive interest, whether it's animals or whatever; secondly, the more concerning thing, is the fact that they can't relate to people. They have no empathy. They walk into a situa-

tion and they are completely lost. Now I don't think Sarah is like that. She's very self-absorbed but I think she does have more understanding than some of the other kids with Asperger's that we've seen. That's why I think the ADHD is the one we should be tackling.

Catherine disagrees:

I think she's got the narrow focus and I think she does misread people. They say that ADHD people don't misread social cues as much as Asperger's, that they just don't pay attention to the cues. I think she does actually misread cues like facial expressions.

Another dilemma for her parents is how to present Sarah's problems to other people, such as teachers at school:

I tell them she's got Asperger's and I can see the teacher looking at me, 'What else are you going to come up with next week? First you're telling me one year it's ADHD and this is it, and then you come back and tell me she's got Asperger's. Well what's going on here?' It's really difficult when you say a child's got two things.

Sarah is in Year 6 at an international school in Singapore. Her last school report had many positive comments from her teachers about both her academic and social progress. Her teachers find her to be a bright, hard-working, enthusiastic, and courteous student. Moving to the school, however, had been very difficult. Sarah had been doing well in her school in Holland with some special needs support and didn't cope well with the move to a new school in an unfamiliar country. She found it very difficult to make friends at her new school and at home was very volatile and sometimes 'explosive.' Her mother describes the move to Singapore and how Sarah reacted:

We moved here and things just went to pieces. Completely. And we had no help from the school. The tantrums happened daily or every second day. She had no friends. She'd walk around the playground apparently with this terrible look on her face. When people tried to make friends with her she'd rebuff them. She was in a lot of grief about leaving Holland, and that's normal. She would hold it in at school, but after school when she got to the car there would be screaming and abuse.

Both Catherine and Peter spoke at length of their frustration with the school for not doing enough to support Sarah and help her settle in. The school failed to acknowledge that Sarah had pre-existing special needs or to appreciate that she was struggling to cope socially with the transition to a new school. Catherine says:

> What got me the angriest about the school is that we had turned up at the school knowing this was going to happen. We knew there was a history of problems. We knew that we needed help. We turned up with a letter from a psychologist at the Dutch school saying this is what needs to be put in place, and they totally ignored it!

Catherine and Peter repeatedly asked to speak with the head of special needs at the school and get some support in place for Sarah. After many months the school finally arranged a meeting. Catherine describes this meeting:

> The head of special needs came in and the first thing she did was a reading test on Sarah. So I said, 'I wanted an interview with you.' And she said, 'I just want to tell you that Sarah is a very bright girl.' I went, 'Yesss – we know that.' And she said, 'Guess what – she's got a reading age of above average.' And I went, 'Yesss.' She said, 'She reads fast, that's really good.' And I said, 'She's got A-D-H-D. We don't want her to read fast! That is an issue – that everything is too fast.' And then I said, 'The issue is that socially this child is just not coping.' She then said, 'That's all right dear they all cope in the end. They all settle down after a while.' And I said, 'This is not a normal situation. This is not a child like everyone else. We've come with an issue, something that existed before we came to this country.'

Sarah now has three very good friends at school. Her mother describes these friendships as genuine and based on a mutual liking of each other's company. While Sarah has had periods without any friends, overall she has managed to have one or two friends that she has been able to keep. In Holland she also had a group of three close friends and seems drawn to being part of a gang of friends. An ongoing issue for Sarah in terms of friendships is to avoid overwhelming her friends so much with her neediness that she loses their friendship. Catherine says:

> She wants her friends 100 per cent of the time. She wants them to not have any other friends. In the past she'd come home from school and want to ring them up straightaway. She'd want to have sleepovers together. It's like nothing was ever enough. So if it's one friend it's just overwhelming. We've talked about it and she's getting better. The other day I said to her, 'Why don't you go and play with Laien after school?' She said, 'Oh because Laien has enough of me at school. She sees me every day. I need to give Laien a break so I won't lose her.'

I interviewed Sarah in the dining room of her house. Unlike many Singaporeans, Sarah doesn't live in a high-rise apartment but in a house in a neighborhood surrounded by woods and walkways. She's a lively, sociable girl who has some good friends who live on her street. At the weekends, she sometimes walks up the road to see if any of her friends want to play. She loves to tell stories while we sit at her dining table, but she sometimes becomes so excited, and talks so fast, that she leaves out key events in the story, or else she scrambles the order in which key events occurred, so that I am left confused and unclear about what actually happened. (I later clarify these stories with her.) There is so much passion and energy in her speech that I am never bored – it's difficult not to be swept away by her enthusiasm. This enthusiasm seems to run through the whole family – both her mum and dad like to talk, and the house has a friendly, inviting, bustling atmosphere. Sarah fidgets as she talks: her hands scramble along the table looking for something to hold on to, twirl, or tap. She likes to have something at hand that she can play with while we speak.

Sarah talks about her life

ADHD and Asperger Syndrome and identity

My mum first talked to me about Asperger's. She was talking about Bill Gates having it, and that got me interested. And then she said that maybe I have it and she started describing things about it, and most of the things she described are what I have – it's so strange! So in the beginning I was excited because Bill Gates is so rich and I said, 'I'm going to become rich!' My brother said, 'Give me a million dollars when you're rich.' So I felt good about it. I haven't told any of my friends about Asperger's because they all know I've got ADHD and because ADHD and Asperger's are nearly the same thing it would be too confusing. I told one friend I had ADHD because I needed to go to the school nurse to get my pills and she had to come with me. Later when she wasn't my friend anymore she told the whole school. So it's like the whole school knows now! And she made it sound like a disease that's catching. One friend even emailed me saying, 'You're just not my type. You're not the kind of friend who I'd hang around with.' At my old school in Holland everyone knew about the ADHD. They thought I was a bit weird but they didn't mind about the weird things I'd do. For example, I would pretend to be a dog at lunchtime. We would be eating for ten minutes and then I would start crawling on the ground under the table for fun. Everyone accepted it.

I was tested for ADHD when I was about seven or eight. My mum thought I acted strangely so I got tested. They put these gluey spots on my head and then put wires on them. I didn't mind. It was like, 'Okay. This explains why I'm weird compared to everyone else – why I'm so different.' I find that I think in different ways. Sometimes instead of finding the hard things hard I find them easy, and I find the easy things hard. I do different stuff and I'm slow in some work and fast in others and I'm slow in growing up, like being into boys and stuff. I also act differently with people. In the past when I got angry I would make growling sounds like a wolf, but every time I did this at school people would think that I was crying so I'd have to say, 'No I'm not crying.' Even now I sometimes growl in anger and people still say that I'm crying.

If I had to describe Asperger's I'd say that it's something like ADHD that you're born with that means you have problems with finding friends, you go 'hyper,' you have to have help with lots of stuff, you learn in different ways, and you have a big interest that you go on about that you never forget. When I found out I had Asperger's I knew why I couldn't have friends that easily, why I liked to make strange noises, and why I was so interested in animals. If I get a new hamster I'll talk and talk about it a lot.

But lately I've also become interested in fantasy and reading fantasy books.

My handwriting is really strange and pretty bad. People just can't seem to understand it. But I can't understand my dad's writing, so I think it's kind of normal. My handwriting *is* bad, but lots of people would think their handwriting is bad compared with other people. My favorite teacher said it doesn't matter too much anyway because in a few years we're all going to be using computers instead of writing on paper. I go to physiotherapy to help with the writing, and for balance and learning to control myself. We throw a ball at the wall and I have to try and catch it. I like it when I get therapy because I get to hold balls and grab on things and try to balance.

I also go to a therapy group with other kids with Asperger's. There are four boys and me. There's a boy called James and he *loves* insects, everything about them. I'm into mammals and birds – I'm not the fish and reptile kind! And he's right into insects and he's going 'Ooh spiders, ooh bats' and all that kind of stuff. I told some of my friends that he was into insects and they said, 'But that sounds like typical boy stuff. Isn't that a normal boy?' And I'm like, 'No this is a bit different!' He's like mad about them. He'll draw a picture of a giant insect squishing a person instead of the other way around – a person squishing an insect. Another boy, Marcus, is really into building things using Lego. Simon likes America. He just goes on and on about America and sometimes computer games. And then there's Jason who likes dinosaurs. Sometimes he yells a lot. He's quite freaky sometimes and he talks about dinosaurs all the time. He has to tell us five facts about dinosaurs before we can even start the lesson.

I like the group. We learn about Asperger's and we do things like drama skits and play games. We talk about what sort of week we've had – the good things that have happened, like going to the water park, and the bad things, like if I've got into trouble or thrown a tantrum. The thing that I really like about the group is seeing people who are like me – other kids who have these big interests. James is funny. He never smiles except if you say 'a giant insect' or something. He just has a frown on his face like all the time and we're like 'Hello! Smile!' It's just so good to feel normal. At school I have to control myself sometimes but in the group I can just be normal, just be myself. My friends at school think the group is for ADHD because they don't know that I have Asperger's.

I think the Asperger's is going down as I get older. The bad things are definitely going down, like the tantrums. The big interest in the animals is going down a tiny bit too because I have to try and control it if I want to have friends. If I keep on talking about animals then I will keep on thinking about them. People don't like it if you only talk about one topic all the time.

Animals, fantasy, and fears

I've been interested in animals my whole life. I like mammals. My favorite animals are dogs and wolves. When I get angry I sometimes even growl like a dog or a wolf. How much do I think about animals? Maybe half the day or quarter of the day cut up into pieces. People tell me to stop thinking about animals!

When I was younger I would make my own animals in my imagination. I'd have a big imaginary eagle called Corix and he'd sit on my shoulder. Once I was climbing a big rock with my mother and when we got to the top it was there, my imaginary horse. It was so real, so solid. When I went on vacation and wasn't able to make any friends I invented animals as friends and I'd use them as fun. Corix came on all our trips. I'd see him flying by the car. At my old school when I was about six and didn't have many friends there either, I would pretend to have a horse and gallop around the school on it. Sometimes I would say, 'I'm an invisible horse.' You'd have to get on top of the horse and you'd see your own feet going so you'd know that it's not exactly there but there in your mind. When I got older my mum told me I had to say the animals were imaginary and not really there and I cried and cried. Even my brother believed me that they were there. I would say that I had a magic calculator that would make any animal come out. It was so sad thinking that they were not really there. Now they are vivid in my mind but they are not there anymore – I don't use them as much as I did before. Sometimes I'll be looking through a book about birds and I'll see a picture of an eagle and I'll think that's the type of bird Corix was.

The things I love the most are animals, adventures, and fantasy. There's a TV show that is my favorite at the moment called *The Wild*

Thornberrys. It's about a girl who can talk to animals and she has adventures with them. Adventures and animals – two of the things I love the best mixed together in one show! Normally I just think and talk about animals all the time, but at the moment I'm more into these fantasy books, the Tamora Pierce series. The first series was about a person trying to become a knight, and the second series was about someone who could talk to animals and then she learnt how to turn into animals. And it was surprising because she just turned into animals and she could turn back and forth and she was a wolf! A wolf for like three weeks!

I have lots of fears. I'm really scared of anything to do with the supernatural – anything that's not true. I'm not scared of anything on this Earth, except maybe snakes, but anything to do with ghosts, devils, and the supernatural really frightens me. There was a concert at school a while back put on by the Year 5 classes. It was called *The Haunted House*. The whole school, even the kindergarten class, was there in the audience watching it. I just couldn't watch it. I sat there for a few minutes and then I just started screaming and had to run out. The other night with my family I watched a movie on TV about a ghost. The movie was called *The Canterville Ghost*. When we went to bed that night I couldn't sleep I was so scared. Mum had to come and sleep with me. I just kept on seeing him – the ghost – walking into my room and it was so scary. Mum said, 'But he was a funny ghost. He was a good ghost.' But it was no use, I just couldn't stop seeing him. I said to Mum, 'Please talk to me. Tell me something to think about so I can get the picture out of my mind.'

Sometimes I have really terrible nightmares. These can go on for days. I remember a few years ago I had a really scary one. My brother Alistair and me were walking across a bridge over a huge canyon and suddenly he fell and died. It was awful. Sometimes I'll have nightmares where people's souls were being removed so that they weren't themselves anymore.

Friends and bullies

A good friend is someone nice who you can trust and who doesn't tell you to do stuff like 'Go and do this for me and I'll give you money' or something. I've got three good friends: Patti, Hiroko, and Laien. We go with Patti to her double bass lessons, but she's very strict about the rules. It's like 'Don't touch the instruments' and we're going 'We're not going to break them!' Hiroko is funny. She plays tag and she likes to make lots of jokes. Laien is one of those intelligent girls. She's the smart one, not really smarter than the rest of us but she does lots of work and smart stuff. She doesn't joke around or get too bossy. She plays with us, games like tag or hide-and-seek. Once when my friend Patti was practicing the double bass we ran up to the room, knocked on the door and ran away!

I met Patti when I was on school camp. At that time I didn't have any friends. We did the sand castles together and played together, and after that we met each other back at school. I knew Hiroko at school but we weren't good friends at first. But later I made friends with her and Laien and we all became good friends. I like playing with my friends at school. Most people think that tag is like a babyish game, but my friends don't and we still like to play it.

I go to Laien's house more than Patti's because she lives just down the street. I've never been to Hiroko's house – it's in Malaysia, but she has come over to my house for a sleepover once. When I go to a friend's place we might play a computer game. Once a friend came over to my place and we made candles. Sometimes we'll just go 'OK what shall we do?' I felt really proud the other day. I went to Laien's house and took my dog along. While I was there I showed her sister how well I had trained Clover. I trained her myself and she's not normally very obedient, even though I say she is. I went 'Sit' and she sat down so quickly! I went 'Go over there' and she went over there! I didn't really think this was going to happen. I felt really proud of how obedient she was.

I have always been teased from kindergarten onwards. I'm used to it now and I've found a new way to cope with it, which is standing up for myself a bit more. The other day my friend and I were looking at a book together and some kids said nastily, 'You're gay.' This time I stood up for myself and said, 'Stop teasing us!' When I was younger they'd not exactly be teasing but they'd say things like 'Sarah, come over here.' And then I'd go in where they'd told me to go and then they'd shout 'Boom!' like the place I had come into had just exploded and I was dead! They'd say I was dead and then they'd run off. It was creepy and I'd cry because I felt so lonely. I just try to be nice to everybody but I guess I must look like a victim to some people. In the past they thought I was a victim because I used to act differently to everyone else but I don't really act that different now. Just when I get angry and growl and they always say 'You're crying' and I'll say 'I'm not crying I'm angry!' I guess that's my weak spot. There are so many things that I've stopped doing now so I won't be teased so much, like crawling on the ground. I've mostly stopped growling, but I might once in a while, once a week maybe, but at one time it was on a daily basis. I've also stopped crying so much – I used to be a cry-baby really. People also used to call me 'goody-goody' because I was always the teacher's pet and I would tell things to the teacher. Then I became less goody-goody and now I'm not. I'm a bit of a goody-goody but not all the time.

Sometimes people can be nasty on the internet. Someone at school secretly copied down my email address when I was giving it to a friend and she must have given it to some other kids and they've been chatting to me on MSN Messenger. It was like lots of rude stuff like saying that I'm a witch and '39% angel, 50% evil...' and strange things like that. In the end I had to block them so they wouldn't chat to me again.

Sensory issues

There are certain things I just can't stand. At the moment I hate saliva. I just hate the touch of it. Other things I hate are hair gel, toothpaste, or anything slimy like that gooey slime that kids play with, the smell of petrol, the feel of those labels at the back of clothes, and woolly clothes. I also hate dolls. I just can't stand their plastic faces. Things like Barbie dolls make me feel gooey and yucky. I look at them and I see goo and I just hate goo. The other day at school we were learning mouth-to-mouth resuscitation and we had to practice on a big plastic doll. I just couldn't do it. I freaked. I just couldn't put my mouth against that cold hard plastic and with that face looking at me.

Tantrums

Sometimes I have tantrums and I get really angry and yell and scream a bit. Every now and then I'll have a really bad one. The last tantrum I had was one of the really bad ones. It was at night-time. I was getting ready for my first day back at school, which was the next day. I was carrying my school clothes – my socks, my undies, and my dress – all in one hand, and in the other hand I was holding a plate. I walked into the living room and my Mum said, 'Tomorrow's sports day!' and she was smiling because she thought 'Oh poor Sarah she's got the wrong clothes.' But I didn't know that at the time and I got really angry because I thought she was being nasty about me having the wrong uniform. So I just dropped the clothes and I tried to get away to be quiet for a while, and then I started screaming and screaming. My brother was in the shower, and when he heard the screams he came running out, and when he ran past me he knocked the plate out of my hand and it broke and I felt angrier and yelled and screamed even more. Mum came in and then there was like a giant argument and I walked out of the house and down to the park. I stayed there for ten minutes until I calmed down. When I was younger I would hurt my mum when she said something that made me angry. I would push her hard against the wall. I can be quite tough.

When I'm having a tantrum I try to calm myself by going to a place for a quiet time. I've been taught to go to a different room and count to ten, moving smoothly, and to stay there for ten minutes. Just basically stay in the room and calm down. If I come out and Mum says something, like anything about having a tantrum, it makes me angry and then I go berserk again and have to go back into the room. I think therapy has helped me learn how to control the tantrums and I think I'm having less of them now.

My future plans

I really enjoy drama, so when I get older I might be an actor. Being an author would also be fun as I like writing. On the other hand I really love animals and I can imagine that in the future I may end up being in a job that involves helping animals in some way, such as taking care of the animals that appear in movies and on TV, or maybe working in a zoo.

CHAPTER 5

Chee Kiong's Story

By being labeled as having Asperger Syndrome people will think that you are less intelligent and that you need more help to do things. People will think that you are slower in learning and that you are not a very friendly person to mix with. That's why I haven't told anybody.

Chee Kiong is 17 years old and was born in Singapore, where he lives with his parents and older brother. Three years ago he was diagnosed with Asperger Syndrome. Like many Singaporean junior college students, his life at present revolves around his studies and preparing for his A-level exams. Outside of academics he is very interested in Japanese anime cartoons and enjoys playing computer games. His parents are proud of his academic achievements but worry about his isolated social life, especially of late as he has not been able to develop any friendships at junior college. After junior college all Singaporean males are required to complete two years' military service, and both Chee Kiong and his family are anxious about how he will cope with the physically taxing combat training, the loud noises of artillery fire, and prolonged social contact with other national servicemen housed in his barracks. Chee Kiong has definite career plans to become a cardiologist, a decision his parents support, and he and his parents are eager for him to begin his university studies. They are petitioning the Ministry of Defense on his behalf and hope that he will be given an administrative position rather than combat training.

According to his parents, Chee Kiong has always been perceived as an unusually quiet boy and didn't speak at all until he was four years old. As a young child he cried a lot and would have massive temper tantrums, often crying solidly for more than an hour. Because he couldn't speak, his parents often relied on guesswork to determine his needs. Chee Kiong's mother Lee Chin recalls this early period:

> When he was age three we were worried that he was deaf or dumb. We sent him to all kinds of specialist doctors. No one could find what was wrong with him. Then one doctor said, 'No need to worry. He's not deaf, not dumb. It's late speech, it happens with some children.' So because I was very worried at that time I stopped working to take care of him. Then I sent him to the nursery because I wanted him to mix with other children so he could pick up language in order to communicate with others.

> By the time he was six he was able to communicate with other children because I had taught him one word at a time when he was young. And then we couldn't teach him any Chinese dialects so we only speak in English, not Mandarin, nothing! No other dialects – it would confuse him. So when we started we were teaching him 'this is a cup, this is a book,' and so on. We started with one word. After three words we would then form a sentence.

Chee Kiong attended speech therapy from the ages of three to six. By the age of five, he was able to use three-word phrases, and by the time he attended school at the age of six he had caught up with his peers and was able to speak in full sentences.

In the early years his parents were also worried about his hyperactive behavior. They consulted a psychiatrist, who then surprisingly prescribed the antipsychotic drug Pericyazine to control his behavior. Chee Kiong's parents were unhappy with the effect of the medication and discontinued it after a week. Lee Chin says:

When he was young he was very hyperactive. He couldn't sit still for five minutes. So the doctor gave him one type of medicine to keep him calm. So an active boy became very inactive, so I worried. He took the medicine for one week and then we stopped. I went back to see the doctor and said, 'I'm not going to give him this type of medicine. I'd rather him be active than a dull boy!'

Lee Chin also recalls that from an early age Chee Kiong showed a lack of interest in his environment and other people. He preferred to play by himself with his own toys, especially his much loved furry soft toys. He would dress up his favorite teddy bears as babies in nappies, and at bedtime he would tuck them up in bed under blankets. Even now Chee Kiong has a huge collection of teddy bears.

At kindergarten Chee Kiong's quietness and passivity were seen as positive characteristics by his teachers. As Lee Chin describes it:

All the teachers liked him so much. They said, 'Oh he's a very good boy. He never fights with other children. He plays by himself and he's very quiet. He never disturbs anyone.'

But this soon changed in primary school where the same characteristics of passivity and quietness seemed to provoke Chee Kiong's classmates into bullying and teasing him. They would call him names and pull faces at him, and every day his lunch money was stolen by the bullies. Lee Chin recalls some of the difficulties during the primary school years and how she and her husband often had to step in and take action:

They bullied him because he was so quiet and he could not socialize with them. One time my husband was very furious. There was this one boy who bullied Chee Kiong so badly until he could not stand it any more. So my husband told the teacher and the Principal. They didn't do anything. One day when school was dismissed, Chee Kiong was very upset and crying. He said, 'Pa, that is the boy that always bullies me.' So my husband went to grab the boy and shook him and told him what would happen if he ever bullied again. After that day the boy dared not bully him again. So his classmates they all said, 'His father, you know, is very fierce. So don't play the fool with him!'

Lee Chin cannot recall her son having any close friends in secondary school. Classmates would sometimes phone him up but usually only to find out about school assignments. Similarly, Chee Kiong's interest in his classmates at that time only really extended to finding out their results on assignments and exams. His mother feels that social problems as opposed to academic problems continue to be the major hurdles in his school life.

> His studies are very good, he has no problems with teachers, he follows rules, learns by himself for his exams. He knows how to do everything in school, he's very well-disciplined. The main thing is that he cannot mix with friends. He doesn't have friends coming around even though we encourage him. For his birthday we asked him, 'Invite your friends, a few friends here then Mum can cook them something good to eat.' But he doesn't want to. He'll say, 'Even if I invited them they might not come.' So I always ask him to at least try. I think he has got a few friends in school now but he says, 'Those friends are not sincere friends.' I just don't know what he means by 'not sincere.'

Chee Kiong is a serious-looking boy who wears thin-rimmed glasses. He speaks carefully and intelligently, weighing his words and monitoring his responses. His face registers little emotion. During our early meetings, he would widen his eyes in response to a question and give me an incredulous look, as if to say, 'How could you even think of broaching such a topic or posing such a question – don't you understand?' It is through this limited gesture that he communicates a type of aloofness. As he grew more comfortable, he opened up, became less wooden in his speech and posture and shared a lot more about himself and his life. He is very focused on his schoolwork and only agreed to be interviewed during the school holidays so as to cause minimum disruption to his homework and revision routine.

Chee Kiong talks about his life

Asperger Syndrome and identity

I was first told that I had Asperger Syndrome about three years ago when I was in secondary school. Even before I had heard of Asperger Syndrome I knew that people thought I was different in some way. Basically I would always go off and do things on my own, and I'm also extremely quiet. I'm very quiet in class and people think that I study too much, but it's not really true. I have always had problems socializing and find it really hard to mix with people. Being able to socialize properly means that you can make friends and you are able to really stick around with these people and do things together. But it happens that when I try to mix with people I find it hard because either I don't understand what they're doing or they don't take me seriously. Sometimes, because of the way I behave, they think of me as being out of the normal and then they treat me like some special person or just isolate me. So because of these problems my parents sent me for psychological tests and they found out I had Asperger Syndrome.

Back then I did not know what autism was, but I soon learned about my condition and that Asperger Syndrome is not a disease but a developmental problem. It affects how the person socializes. The person cannot socially develop or communicate effectively and needs help with how he socializes and how he makes friends. When you want people with Asperger Syndrome to make friends they don't really make friends, rather they hang around groups and try to mix. But the thing is they don't know how to interact in the first place. So you can't say they are socializing. That is the problem.

When I first found out I had Asperger Syndrome I had mixed feelings. I was quite confused about myself and also a bit disappointed because I realized that because of this problem I can't socialize with people properly. It was stopping me from doing things. The reason why I felt really confused is that I wasn't sure whether I was *really* different from normal people. But then I realized that autistic people are almost the same as normal people – it's just that they can't socialize. When I found out about my Asperger Syndrome I found out that it was a mild disorder, so in many ways I am actually luckier than other people but I still need help to improve, to socialize with people, to be more creative in the way I do things, and also to be more sensible in the ways I behave. I don't think that I will outgrow this – Asperger Syndrome will still be with me – it's just that it keeps improving. Things haven't really changed for me since I've found out I have Asperger Syndrome but I do know more about myself and I know there are other people who are just like me. I do see it as being a disability and one that stays with you for your whole life. But you can't cry and grieve over this problem because it's there with you forever. You can't take it away. If I could change myself and get rid of the Asperger Syndrome then I definitely would.

Sometimes people with Asperger Syndrome do unusual things on their own account because their mind is not really focused on what they are doing. Because of this other people see them as abnormal. I always make sure that I know what I am doing so that I don't do silly things in public, such as speaking too loudly in the library. I'm very careful. I was told that I must be aware of what I do because if I do silly things then I may attract people's attention, which is unnecessary. I saw it happen to someone once when I was studying in the library. I was searching the net for information and then this guy, who also has Asperger Syndrome, suddenly said the words 'Bill Clinton' for no reason. I continued doing my work and then a few minutes later he blurted out loudly 'Bill Clinton' again! And I wondered to myself why he did that.

People sometimes think that people with AS have special abilities but I don't think that's true. The reason why they appear to excel is because they have a strong interest in one thing: they concentrate, put all their effort into doing this one thing, and try to find each and every single detail about it. Basically I've never found anything in myself that is a special ability. I used to do really well in maths but then I realized that I'm not really the best in maths. For example, when I entered junior college I found out there was a guy who was really lazy who had scored 82/100 on a maths test. I got a really weird result for that same test, 61/100, even though I knew all the methods. I did badly because of carelessness, and I felt so angry and jealous that this really lazy person did so much better than me.

I don't like to tell people that I have Asperger Syndrome. It's a personal thing. It's very confidential because I know that people at school are very gossipy and if I were to tell them about my personal problems they would start to spread rumors about me. I couldn't accept that. Also not many people know about this condition; they still view it as a mental abnormality, which is just not true. I feel that the way society views autistic people is not right. They think that autistic people are hopeless cases, that they are mentally abnormal people who can't be changed or saved, which is just not true. There's always some hope in everything. By being labeled as having Asperger Syndrome people will think that you are less intelligent and that you need more help to do things. People will think that you are slower in learning and that you are not a very friendly person to mix with. That's why I haven't told anybody.

When I was at secondary school we never told my teachers about my condition. When I started junior college I didn't want to tell the teachers, but my mother said, 'You can't hide this anymore.' She wanted to make sure that I got help when I needed it and that I had someone to talk to about my problems at school. So she told the Principal and my form teacher. In the end I felt quite relieved that they knew. We sent a report to the Principal and she is a very responsible, kind, and caring person. As a result she said to the teachers, 'This particular person has this particular problem so please help him.'

Asperger Syndrome and socializing: Searching for sincerity

The worst problem for me in my life is socializing. I cannot make friends and I need friends badly. When you have friends you get more support and you can ask a lot of things from them and they'll help because they're your friends. You also gain a lot of knowledge and experience from your friends. And because I don't have friends it means that I'm cut off from help. Whenever I have a problem I have to handle it on my own. I don't know how to socialize and that means I don't know how to use people to my advantage. To me that is the biggest problem with having Asperger Syndrome.

The most difficult thing about school is how I interact with people. I just can't get it right. Sometimes I ask people questions, but because of the way that I ask the question they think, 'This person is very strange.' I feel very strongly about what people think of me, their impression of me. My classmates have always thought of me as someone who loves doing homework, a workaholic, and they find it very unpleasant. And also because I don't talk very much they think of me as too quiet. So the thing is I'm very isolated; I'm very left out. Lunch breaks are hard. I don't know many people, so usually I don't do much except eat. After eating my lunch I will usually just sit and read.

My classmates look down on me. They look down on people who are not so trendy. They think of me as mature and outdated. I always talk about things that they don't like. They talk about hand-phone [mobile phone] models – so-called fashionable things, but I don't see why fashion is so important. Fashion is fashion and whether you want to follow it is your business. You can't look down on people who are outdated. I feel narrow-minded people should change, and that's why I don't really like my classmates. Basically they are rowdy and spread rumors about me. This is a big problem because they are indirectly making me appear to be antisocial by telling lies about me and cutting off my relationships with other people. They'll tell outrageous lies, for example that I smoke or I insult teachers – and this is the most absurd one – that I have a girlfriend and that I rape her. This is so stupid and untrue, but then people hear it and think I'm a really bad person. Once people have a bad impression it's really hard to change that. So no matter how much I try to tell them that I am innocent and that these people are telling lies, nobody wants to believe me.

The head prefect makes me angry. The teachers expect him to be very responsible and upright, but he's really immature. And the strangest thing is that he gets the top grades in class. I feel he doesn't deserve this because his attitude is not right. The way he behaves really disappoints me. If you asked any student they would say, 'Oh prefects are better than normal students because not only are they very good at studies but they can also discipline other students.' But I don't think prefects are any better than anybody else. Since Secondary 3 I've come across some school prefects who have abused their authority. They've poked their fingers into my letters and personal stuff during recess and then they've spread rumors about me. Every time this has happened I've complained to the teacher, but then the prefect has lied and said, 'I didn't do that.' They're seen as role models and so people believe them.

I know my classmates in junior college don't like me. It's so sad but I haven't made any friends at all at JC this year. Back in both primary and secondary school at least I had a small group of friends, but in JC I don't have any because everyone seems to be so selfish. All they are interested in are paper qualifications and being number one. For them studying is like a rat race. They think I'm proud – a nerd and a loner who thinks he knows everything – but they are wrong. I'm not as cocky as they think I am. In fact in my class there are other people who are a lot prouder and cockier. The ones who do better than me academically like to verbally abuse me. Sometimes they'll even vandalize my name in the lecture theaters. They'll write 'Chee Kiong sucks' or 'Chee Kiong loves so and so.' It's just so stupid and antisocial.

When I was younger, people took advantage of me because I complied with them. If they said 'I want you to do this or that' then I would just do it. For some odd reason I was a very easy target to be picked on in this way. But I later realized that I can think for myself and I don't have to follow other people. I was teased a lot when I was in Primary 5 and 6. I was with the same group of students for both years and they teased me and made me an outcast. In effect I was put in exile. They'd call me 'mute' because I didn't talk a lot. It makes me really angry now because most of the things that these children said back then were wrong; they judged too quickly and stereotyped people. It seems that people like me, who always know the answers, who read a lot and who are alone, are going to be labeled 'nerds.' I think primary school children really show their age, they are really childish.

I do have one friend at the moment but he's still at secondary school and not at my JC. I only met him about six months before I left secondary school. I still make contact with him but not as often. When I first met him he also appeared to be very lonely and I thought he seemed very smart. I approached him very modestly at first and asked: 'Which class are you from?'; 'What's your name?'; 'What are your interests?' We met for a while and once I was very sure and confident that he was somebody I could be friends with, I started sharing my interests with him and he seemed to appreciate it. So we began to exchange personal things with each other and that's when we became friends. It felt good because I find it hard to meet people who are honest and sincere. To me, a good friend is someone who doesn't lie and who isn't insincere or dishonest. It is someone who shares things, their interests – not just knowledge or how to do homework.

I also sometimes get emails from friends. During the first few months of junior college I met this guy who goes to another JC and he sends me an email about once a week. He often draws sketches and passes them on to me. Because he is intelligent I asked him questions about physics and maths, but I don't think he liked it and somewhere along the line he said, 'We don't have to send mail on a work basis.'

I'm not dating at the moment. The girls know that I'm not as charming as the other boys. They find me very lonely and very quiet – very individualistic. I think they think of me as a typical Singaporean male who is very uncool and lacking in sexual appeal. Because they don't have a good impression of me, there's no reason to ask them out for dates. I think that I should be conservative and wait until I'm older, once I get a job and am more stable, before I start to date. Maybe then I can find a partner that I can trust. There's no point just simply looking for some beautiful girl to say 'I love you' to and then later on getting a divorce. I know that I'm the type of person who doesn't take risks, so I'll wait until I'm older.

Grades, homework, and exams

School work and homework are *really* important to me. I feel great when I get good results in exams and tests. When I was in my first year in secondary school I got 99 out of 100 for my end of year mathematics exam, and for science I was actually the top of the whole class. The interesting thing is that we expect everyone in the class to compete with each other but it's quite easy in the first year. So I was the so-called top boy in the class and I think my classmates were jealous. Now that I'm in junior college I'm competing with better students.

I do feel worried about not living up to expectations. Because I've achieved something very good in the past, people expect more – that I'll get full marks, be the top in the class, the top boy. So in a way I have to force myself to be a perfectionist. But when I don't achieve my minimum expectations, which are usually too high, I get disappointed. For example, I was very disappointed in Secondary 4 because I did okay in my preliminary exams but in the end I didn't get very good final grades. I was acting like I was going to get A1s but instead I got B3s and A2s and so I had to ask myself, 'Where did I go wrong?' I think it was because I was very careless in the exams. I don't know if I was just too confident or just nervous but my carelessness really put down my marks quite a lot. In my science papers there were lots of calculation errors. I most probably did the paper too quickly, assuming that I knew everything.

Exams can be a problem for me. During lessons I contribute a lot by answering the teacher's questions. The thing is, when it comes to exams I can't answer that well because exams test other kinds of skills – you're not just simply recalling facts. They want you to apply the information, and students who can apply the facts do better than the ones who only memorize everything. Understanding exam questions is another problem for me. If the question is structured a little bit differently from my revision notes then it takes me a lot of time to read and understand the question. But because there is so much time pressure in exams, I usually end up reading the question too quickly and not fully understanding it, and this leads to mistakes. It really makes me angry, because I know I am intelligent and I know the concepts well. I ask myself, 'Why is it that other students who are supposed to be less intelligent than me do better?' I feel like I've been indirectly insulted when I don't do that well in a test.

I have this habit – that I've had for a long time – that I must do my homework immediately so that I'll have more time to do revision. If I have more time to do revision then maybe I will get more A grades. If I have any free time at school I will probably start doing my homework. This is one thing that is very different about me: other people at school hang out in groups and chit-chat and socialize and have fun at school and do their homework at home. I think we should do our homework at school not at home because it is simply not true that we can concentrate better at home. In fact, I feel we are more likely to be lazier at home. We should work longer hours in the library where we can, if necessary, discuss any questions or problems with the teachers. I've always wanted to do my homework straightaway, because I'm very slow and need lots of time if I want the work to be perfect, neatly written, and with well-organized answers. The extra time required, of course, means doing some of the homework at school and then the moment I get home I'll do the rest of my homework immediately. The junior-college teachers are also very demanding and in fact actually grade your homework. In the past in secondary school and primary school they didn't grade homework, they just checked to see if you had done it correctly.

Teachers: Compliance and contempt

Teachers are human beings, so they have their own biases, but I have no trouble talking to them because I basically find it easier to socialize with more mature people. I had one teacher in my junior college who was friendlier towards me than to the other students because he saw that I listened to him and took notes. Basically, if he had any questions, minor things like what time it is, or if he needed to borrow a dictionary when he didn't have his, then he would always approach me first. I do remember having difficulty mixing with some teachers who didn't like the way I behaved. These teachers thought I was too hard-working and a nerd. You know the stereotype – people who read lots of books, who study all the time, who wear glasses, don't exercise a lot, and talk a lot of rubbish. My geography teacher in secondary school definitely thought I was a nerd. I had her for four years for English and geography. She liked those students who were smart but didn't work hard, who lied and manipulated other people and who played power games – these students had the qualities she admired. If you want to put it in Chinese dialect she was a real *Ah Lian*. In Singapore we call certain Chinese ladies who speak very loudly and in broken English *Ah Lians*. They are very rough and lacking in courtesy. This is how she described herself too. Basically, she was saying if people are very gentle then they have a slim chance of making friends with her. She always thought I was sleepy in class because I like to do my work with my head close to the desk, so she would come over and bang on my desk really loudly. It used to make me feel extremely upset. She thought she was waking me up, but I was already awake. She didn't understand me, so I don't blame her for her behavior. At the time though, I was so angry I wanted to hit her; but I knew that violence wasn't going to solve the problem, so I just kept quiet and let her have her own way. In Secondary 2 I had an art teacher who was even worse. This teacher only liked females; she thought girls are better artists and better behaved. I still see her sometimes when she is invigilating an exam I am sitting and she'll come in and praise the girls and insult the boys.

Sensory issues

For some weird reason I really dislike the look and feel of Plasticine. The color always looks very unnatural to me especially when you mix different colors together and you get a color that is brownish and very dirty looking. I also don't like the smell of it. In my opinion it's slightly pungent and smelly. Strong smells really bother me, and that's why I hate the wet market. I always pinch my nose when I enter a wet market. I guess its natural that a wet market would smell because of the smell of fresh meat and vegetables. The water there is dirty and impure and the thing is I don't like dirty things and I'm very afraid of really bad smells.

National service

I'm very worried about doing national service (NS) because I'm not used to that sort of environment. The environment in NS is not pleasant like at home: it's very harsh and people will just simply scold you for doing something silly. I know that sometimes I do really stupid things and sometimes I don't follow instructions that well, so I'm afraid that I will be punished a lot. Also in NS you have to deal with all kinds of people. In junior college or in school we are protected in the sense that we generally only meet people who are similar to us in their qualities and their mindsets. They are studious. But not all the people in NS are going to be like that. You will get people who are gangsters, people who are school drop-outs, even some who didn't go to school at all. So in national service you will meet people that you wouldn't normally meet – people who speak Chinese dialects in a very rough manner. I'll have to get used to these things and it will be very hard for me to adjust.

My future plans

After finishing my two years of national service I am hoping to study medicine at the National University in Singapore. Ideally I would like to be a specialist in cardiology. Cardiology is about the human heart, and to me the heart is the most important organ in the body, even more so than the brain. This is my primary ambition for the near future.

CHAPTER 6

Luke's Story

I do want to give people with Asperger's a more realistic identity. Normal or neurologically typical people are taken as individuals, whereas I've found that with Asperger Syndrome you get this perception of 'Asperger people.' We are always a group, you know, like clones.

Luke is 14 years old and the author of two successful books on Asperger Syndrome (Jackson 2001, 2002). He lives in the North of England with his family: his mother Jacqueline, and his three brothers and three sisters, Matthew (19), Rachel (17), Sarah (15), Anna (12), Joseph (9), and Ben (6). Joseph has been diagnosed with ADHD and Ben with autism. Luke attends a local private secondary school.

Luke's mother Jacqui noticed when Luke was very young that he was different from other children his age. Luke would flap his arms and he developed unusual and obsessive interests, including collecting batteries and pencils and playing with string. The turning point came when Luke was asked to leave kindergarten after only a few days for acting aggressively towards the other children. Kindergarten staff suggested that Luke be assessed by the local Autistic Research Team, who subsequently diagnosed Luke with Asperger Syndrome. Luke was the first in his family to be diagnosed with an autism spectrum disorder, although later his youngest brother Ben would be diagnosed with autism. Jacqui notes that at that time there was little in the way of therapies available locally for Luke so she started to research AS herself, learning about various strategies commonly used with children on the autistic spectrum such as 'social stories.' When he started school, the Autistic Research Team people were in the background, monitoring and supporting as needed. Luke saw an occupational therapist but, according to Jacqui, the level of occupational therapy was very basic and not really tailored to Asperger's.

Luke has always attended mainstream schools. Jacqui says that few alternatives in the way of appropriate special schools are available in their city.

> It's a really strange set up in a way. We have a school for profound and multiple learning difficulties, a moderate learning difficulties school, and mainstream. That's it. Nothing exists that is specifically geared towards kids with Asperger's where you can also do all your GCSEs. Luke's always liked the idea of going to a special school but not if it means being restricted to doing only a limited number of GCSEs.

Jacqui also feels that a potential problem with special schooling is social isolation.

> Even if there was a school where all the curriculum was geared towards kids with AS and you could do all your GCSEs, it would still be very isolating. The moment you're out of school there are all these typical, normal people waiting to chomp at your ankles, figuratively speaking, and you're not prepared.

In his book *Freaks, Geeks and Asperger Syndrome* (2002) and in his interviews with us Luke says that he dislikes school and pretty much lives for after school and the weekends. Sadly, school seems to be a necessary evil to be got through. Luke has always been bullied at school, and this naturally colors his feelings. In Jacqui's words:

> He's been bullied ever since he went to school. The school's answer has usually been 'that's just what kids do.' He's had that since he was three and it has been constant. Sometimes I'll try and stop the bullying by going into the school and speaking

with the kid, the teachers, and the parents. Then he'll have six weeks' break where it's easier and then it'll start all over again. And then the last school when he moved from primary into secondary school was disastrous. He just couldn't get over the bullying.

Jacqui withdrew Luke from his last school because of the bullying, and he is presently attending a private secondary school that has smaller classes. The situation with bullying has improved at this school, though Luke is still socially isolated. Jacqui says that Luke doesn't really have any school friends and that the kids' perception of him is that he is 'weird' or 'freaky.'

> Even with his older brother and sisters not a day goes by without one of those saying to him something like 'God you're such a freak!' One of the reasons is that he doesn't have the theory of mind to know that other people can't read his mind so he'll just suddenly stand up and say a random sentence and expect people to know what it relates to. He's obviously thinking about that particular thing and he presumes we all know what's he's thinking about.

Similarly, Jacqui says that social skills such as making conversation can be difficult for Luke and can accentuate this image of someone who is odd.

> A conversation with Luke might go like this:
>
> 'How are you Luke?'
>
> 'Oh I'm fine, a little tired.'
>
> 'Why's that?'
>
> 'Oh last night my computer crashed and I was up all night…'

And to be polite and make conversation the other person will ask what sort of program Luke's running and then bang he's in and he'll go on and on about megahertz and gigabytes and what not. Every single conversation ends up being about computers, which of course bores people and their eyes start to glaze over. Kids of his own age group just think he's weird and the adults just tend to stand there with fixed smiles while he goes on about HTML.

Jacqui is concerned that Luke may be feeling depressed due to his lack of friendships. Luke, however, doesn't describe himself as being particularly depressed, although he acknowledges that there are days when he feels miserable for no particular reason. When speaking with us he also found it very difficult to recall times when he's felt especially happy. Jacqui says a related issue is that Luke's body language probably doesn't express what he's truly feeling:

> Joe and I can be in silly moods and we're jumping around the place having fun. Whereas Luke could quite easily be feeling exactly as Joe and I are but he'll be sitting there on the computer with exactly the same face as if he wasn't feeling like that. His face isn't always appropriate.

In *Freaks, Geeks and Asperger Syndrome* Luke strongly advises parents to tell their children sooner rather than later that they have AS. Luke himself was told by his mother that he had Asperger's when he was 12 and was initially very angry with her for waiting so long to tell him. He describes in his book the immense relief he felt when he first heard that he had AS:

> I had finally found the reason why other people classed me as weird. It was not just because I was clumsy and stupid. My heart lightened instantly and the constant nagging that accompanied me all my life (not my mum) stopped immediately. I finally knew why I felt different, why I felt as if I was a freak, why I didn't seem to fit in. Even better, it was not my fault! (p.34)

> Although a child may go through a period of asking questions or being angry and upset, in my mind that is still no excuse not to tell them…you are not protecting them because feeling as if you are a 'freak' is horrible at any time and much worse when you don't know the reason why. (p.37)

Luke works hard to promote a greater understanding of AS. As well as his books, he has been interviewed by BBC radio and was featured in the BBC TV documentary *My Family and Autism*, which aired in July 2003 (he even shot some of documentary footage himself). He has also been an

invited speaker at a number of autism and AS conferences in the UK.
Both Luke and his mother – who works as a helpline volunteer for
Allergy Induced Autism (AiA) – advocate the benefits of trying a glu-
ten-free/casein-free diet for those with an ASD. Jacqui first tried the diet
on the family after keeping a food diary for her son Joseph, who was suf-
fering from a bowel condition. She noticed he behaved more erratically
after he ate foods containing gluten and casein. Luke believes that,
although the diet was initially difficult because of uncomfortable with-
drawal symptoms, the benefits outweigh the initial discomfort as it has
brought an end to the interminable stomach pain he once suffered and
has made his daily life more manageable.

A major source of tension between Luke and his mother is the amount
of time he spends on the computer. This interest is so consuming that
Jacqui likens it to an addiction. She feels that it definitely interferes with
his studies and his relationships within the family:

> Luke doesn't really do books, he doesn't do video and he
> doesn't do movement! He doesn't do anything whatsoever but
> sit there on the computer. There's one game – Runescape – that
> he's been playing for about six months now and he's on that 16
> hours a day in the weekends and holidays. On school days he'll
> walk in the door, drop his school bag, sit on the computer and go
> on Runescape. I'll say, 'Luke haven't you got any homework?'
> He won't acknowledge me. Half an hour later I'll say it again. I
> have to physically drag him off. He'll eat his dinner and then get
> back on Runescape again.

Jacqui says that his school work has suffered because of his obsession
with the game:

> Before becoming obsessed with Runescape his grades were in
> the 80 per cent and 90 per cent range. Since Runescape his
> grades have now dropped to the 30 per cent range in most
> subjects except English, where he still gets grades in the 90s.

Jacqui has been trying to divert his attention away from Runescape by
encouraging him to explore other more creative aspects of computing
such as HTML programming:

At least if he's stuck on that he's learning something and there's some benefit to it. I'd say with Runescape it's on within three seconds of him walking through the door and it's still on at midnight. You can't get him to go to bed. You'll start saying at nine o'clock, 'Come on Luke it's bed time,' and then at eleven o'clock he's still on it. It's one big takeover and there's no benefit to it.

Jacqui feels that the time spent on Runescape has also recently affected how he interacts with his brothers and sisters and that he now sees his family as an annoying distraction that costs him time away from the computer. Jacqui is worried that the obsession may affect Luke's future plans, such as studying at university: 'There are lots of possibilities for the future. It's just that at present the first priority is that we have to find some way of steering him off Runescape.'

We spoke with Luke in his living room at home with his mother close by and often joining in with the conversation. Luke and his mother seem close and often spar with each other in a joking way over a difference in opinion or recollection of an anecdote. Luke's brothers and sisters often pop into the living room during the interviews and the house has a busy and active atmosphere. Luke is often reticent about talking about himself and sometimes comes across as self-deprecating. For example, he modestly downplays his impressive achievement of authoring two books at such a young age. Similarly, it's only after a lot of detailed questioning about his computer skills that he speaks of his websites, the bulletin board he has created for his gaming clan, and his experience with Linux. He has a keen wit and every so often lightens our conversation with a well-phrased sardonic remark or joke. He has a narrow range of interests, revolving mainly around computers, and doesn't seem to have any close friends with whom to share these interests. He has been learning Taekwondo for a number of years although his current preoccupation with computer games seems to have overshadowed his interest in the sport. Luke is a prolific reader and will often start and complete a book in one night. He likes to read fantasy novels, such as those by Terry Pratchett, which he says are commonly popular with people with Asperger's: 'Every single Asperger's person I've ever met has read and liked Terry Pratchett. It could be used in the diagnostic criteria!' He is very knowledgeable about Asperger Syndrome and the GF/CF diet and is involved in the autism/AS professional circuit as a spokesperson.

Luke talks about his life

Asperger Syndrome and identity

I first found out about Asperger Syndrome when I was 12. Around that time an article on AS appeared in *The Guardian* and Mum had strategically placed the newspaper on the floor knowing that I would pick it up and read it. The article talked about the various symptoms of AS and different people who had AS such as Einstein. Einstein wasn't actually diagnosed as having AS, but the article said he had all the traits. In those days I suppose it was just thought of as being eccentric. After reading the article I went over to Mum and said, 'Mum I've got all of these traits, what's this all about?'

'Well yeah,' she said rather nonchalantly, 'you've got AS.'

'Oh thanks for telling me!'

At first it didn't really sink in. I thought, 'Whoa I can't have this because I'm just me.' It all felt a bit unreal and I wanted it to be proven to me somehow with medical tests or something. At school it was quite weird initially because I started comparing myself to the other kids and perceiving everything they do as normal. They just seemed to get on with each other more and not do some of the odd things that I do. I find it quite difficult to distinguish which bits of my personality are AS traits and which bits are just me. I usually try to sort it out by observing NTs (neuro-typicals) – I know that term can be offensive – and seeing how they are different from me. I just accept AS now and gradually it's become a part of my life.

I'm the author of two books on AS. My most recent book is about my experiences as a teenager with AS. The kids at school know that I've written this book but none of them have read it. I don't think they would understand it properly anyway. The reaction has been along the lines of, 'Are you that boy who has that disease and has written a book about it?' So they all think Asperger's is like some big disease. After the books came out I became quite involved with AS, being interviewed by the media and speaking at conferences and so on. I wouldn't say I'm a campaigner for

AS – I'm not walking around with signs like 'Save the whales' – but I do want to give people with Asperger's a more realistic identity. Normal or neurologically typical people are taken as individuals, whereas I've found that with Asperger Syndrome you get this perception of 'Asperger people.' We are always a group, you know, like clones. We get generalized a lot: AS people are like this; this is what AS people do. You have to fit a certain description. For example, you have to have difficulties making friends, look down at the floor all of the time, wave your hands in the air, and so on. It's like every symptom has to be ticked off. But it isn't really like that – people can't be labeled as easily as that. We're not clones.

Another misconception is that it is a disease – a terminal illness or something. It's a very negative view and I feel that as well as the bad bits there are a lot of good things associated with having Asperger's. Sometimes I do think, 'God why do I have to have it?' but for me the good points of having AS outweigh the bad. I do find it really hard to socialize, but on the plus side I find it easier to concentrate than normal people. I have some sensory issues – for example, I hate the feel of sand and cotton wool – but I'm really able to focus on my interests, such as computers, and I know I'll be able to get a job in that area. You can work on the bad aspects of AS and manipulate the good aspects to your advantage. I've also noticed that some of the negative aspects are getting better over time. Things like understanding facial expressions improve as you get older because to some extent you can learn them. I think as you get older you realize that there are certain things that people don't do and if you go ahead and do these things then people will think you are a bit strange and won't like you.

When I was younger I used to be more obviously unusual. For one thing, I used to wear a balaclava day and night, which is kind of like having a headlight on your head! I'd walk into a bank and everyone would duck! I don't think anyone at school actually knew what my face looked like until about Year 6. I stopped wearing it when I was about ten. We used a star chart to get me to stop. If I took the balaclava off at meals, I would get a star; and by the end of the week I would have enough stars to get a treat. If I took it off while I was watching TV, I would get a gold star; and after I got a certain number of gold stars I would get an even bigger treat. Eventually wearing the balaclava petered out to nothing.

I'm often interviewed by the media and speak at conferences. I think I must have traveled to London about 17 times for various events. The last speech I gave was for my publisher's 15th anniversary celebration where I spoke for over ten minutes – this is the longest speech I have ever given. It took a lot out of me and I was in a bit of a bad mood afterwards. Now I'm being filmed for a BBC documentary. They want me to shoot some amateur video at school, which is quite annoying for the other kids. I have to film about two tapes. I don't mind doing these things too much because at least there are more people learning about AS and more people going on the gluten-free/casein-free (GF/CF) diet which my family and I strongly believe in. My first book was about the benefits of this diet for people with AS and ADHD.

After I started on the GF/CF diet, all my stomach pains went. I had experienced stomach pains all my life, but when the withdrawals from the diet started the pains were a thousand-fold worse. After the withdrawals had finished, the pains got completely better and my face improved too: I didn't have black rings around my eyes and permanently red ears. I used to glow like a traffic light! One of the reasons people don't stay with the diet is the effect of the withdrawals that usually happen about nine weeks into the diet. For example, parents will say, 'Oh the diet doesn't work. My ADHD kid's even worse now. He's really bad news – he's just trashed the place!' But that's actually a good reaction, because it means that once the withdrawals are over he will react in a good way to the diet.

I have to stick to the diet very strictly. A lot of parents will say, 'My child's really bad today and I don't know what's wrong. He's only had one biscuit today.' But you're not supposed to give them a few biscuits, not even a few crumbs. For example, we have different peanut butter because even a few stray crumbs in the jar will drive my brother Joe loopy and give me agonizing stomach pains. For lunch at school I usually take a packed meal from home. We eat these little corn cakes instead of sandwiches; they taste nice but are quite annoying because they are low-fat so they hardly fill you up at all.

Computer games and obsessions

I really love computers. I think about them and talk about them a lot. When I talk to people the conversation always seems to wander to computers, because that's what I'm really interested in. Mum thinks I'm definitely obsessed on them. I started to play on the old Spectrum computers before I could even read. To start a game on a Spectrum you'd have to type the command for the game that you wanted to play and then it would load it and you'd be able to play. We got a PC when I was about four or five. First of all I was just interested in games, but then I actually started messing around with the internal workings of the PC. I kept wondering how the games worked and what went on inside the computer. A few times I stuffed up Mum's computer a little bit! I remember once there was a huge uproar because I crashed Mum's computer and we couldn't get it started again. Mum shouted, 'LUKE!' and I ran off and hid in the bedroom! At present, I'm still keen on fiddling with all the menus and themes on the PC. Mum complains that every time she goes on the computer there's a different screensaver, a different color scheme and fonts, and a different backdrop!

For the last six months I've been playing this online role-playing game called Runescape. Mum's a bit upset about it because she thinks that I play it too much. During the week I reckon that I play for about two hours a day but during the weekends and school holidays I can play up to 16 hours a day. In the game you create a character that goes on a quest in an imaginary land. You can choose what character you want to be, such as a monk, a miner, or a warrior. I have two characters: Sir Tainly and Sir Loin Steak. I mainly play Sir Tainly who is a miner and a smith, which is good because it means he can make his own armor. Mum thinks I have become obsessed with the game and now have less interest in going out, doing Taekwondo, reading, playing with my brother Joe, or studying! She thinks I play it every spare minute of the day. In the game you can join up with other players to form a 'clan' which is a group of players who play together. I've even started my own clan and built a computer bulletin board so that we can post messages to one another. Our characters get together online and go on quests. I don't really consider the clan to be friends. Even though we talk to each other online, we haven't seen each other and we only talk about the game. I like the game because it's a bit like real life, except it's easier.

I know how to program a web page in HTML and sometimes I just get immersed in programming. I've tried Linux, especially Red Hat Linux. You can change anything on that operating system. But it's hard to understand – it's even hard to install a basic program because everything is in C++ and source codes. When I do coding it tends to be in HTML. I'm making a website at the moment that will be a collection of simple HTML lessons. I'm thinking of calling it 'Tutorial Script,' 'Tutorial Tech,' or 'Tutorial Soft.' Some of my favorite subjects at school are IT and computer-aided design.

Asperger Syndrome and socializing: Not being part of the pack

I don't really have much social instinct, and because of that I do find it hard to socialize. My sister once asked me, 'Who do you hang around with?' and I was like, 'What do you mean hang around with?' It took me ages to figure out what 'hang around' means, but I now know it's all a part of being social, like speaking with people on the phone and going to clubs, and so on. I don't hang around with anyone really. The downside is that I do get a bit lonely, but most of the time I see no reason to hang around in these big wolf packs. And I've never seen any reason to just speak to people on the phone unless I've got something specific to speak to them about. My sister can chat away for hours on the phone with her friends. She's like, 'Oh my god, oh, he didn't! He did? No!' It's just like those American sitcoms. I find it utterly stupid, to be honest.

Social situations like discos and parties are really difficult for me. These situations seem to come easily to normal people, but I just don't know what to do and where to put myself. I know there are certain social rules but I never seem to instinctively know them, such as who I am meant to talk to at a party and for how long and when to move on to the next group of people. My conversations always seem to wander to the topic of computers. Sometimes by the end of the evening I feel like everyone is glaring at me and I never actually know why, which is a bit annoying.

If I could change one thing about myself I would make myself a bit more social. I'd like to be able to go to discos and parties without feeling really uncomfortable. The last party I went to was about two years ago and I've only ever been to two school discos in my whole life. The first one was fun but the second one was absolute hell. It was noisy and everywhere I looked something was flashing at me. All the people were crowding in and in the end I found myself so bored that I was actually picking up rubbish from the floor for the cleaner.

There's a lot of pressure to be social. I find it weird how people want me to be a 'normal' person rather than just accept me for who I am. One of my teachers is an example of this attitude.

'Have you been socializing lately, Luke?'

'Yes, sir, just hanging around with a friend called Matt.'

'Oh, so you've made a friend now. That's really good!'

He means well but it's quite annoying that he assumes that I should be outside with the boys playing rugby and that I'm miserable because I prefer to spend my lunchtimes alone in the computer lab.

My friends at the moment are Peter and Matt. Peter has Asperger's, but he's quite different to me. He's very hyper, bouncing around all over the place, whereas I'm a lot more focused. Peter used to go to my school but he left recently. I see Peter once every two or three weeks and we'll usually go to the pictures on a Saturday. Matt is at my school. He hasn't been diagnosed with Asperger's but he's definitely got some of the traits. He's very obsessed with trains and he's quite routine bound. We both like talking about computers and things. But he's trying really hard to fit in with the popular crowd and because I'm considered to be uncool he said that we can only be friends outside of school. He thinks his reputation would be ruined if the other kids saw him talking to me.

At school there's a lot of talk about who's going out with whom and people flirting with each other, but getting a girlfriend isn't really a high priority for me at the moment. I can't say that it preys on my mind – I've never really followed the crowd and thought I must do this because everyone else is doing it. I think it's stupid to be different to everyone else just for the sake of being different, but then again it's also stupid to try to fit a specific social status. I also don't think it's an issue as I doubt any girl would actually go out with me anyway. I just don't think I'm boyfriend material.

School and bullies

If I had to rate my happiness on a scale from one to ten, with ten being the highest, I'd say about three on weekdays and nine at weekends. School definitely makes me unhappy. I hate all the moving from classroom to classroom and all the social stuff. You have to be a certain way to fit into the social group and I find that really hard. And then there are all the people who just think that you are the scum of the earth, and the bullies who just put you down completely.

I've been bullied ever since I started school. It was really awful at my last school as I was quite often kicked and punched. After one really bad incident my Mum took me out of the school for good. That particular time I got punched up and tormented so badly that I had to run out of the school to get away from the bullies. I was walking up the road when I saw them hiding behind a billboard waiting for me, so I changed direction and went into the nearby swimming baths and hid there. My mum had to come and pick me up. I never went back to that school.

I've also had a long experience of being called names: 'freak,' 'geek,' and any other you care to mention. They don't actually bother me because they're only names. I think the reason why I get bullied is because I'm different and don't find it easy to socialize. I'm in a private school now and it's definitely better in terms of the bullying, but I still really hate school. I mostly hang around by myself. At the moment there's a kid in my class who's always slagging me off to make everyone laugh at me. He's sort of like the Messiah in the class and he's really popular because he's so clever. He went forward one year so he's only 12 when everyone else in the class is 13 and he's got an IQ of about 160 or something really huge.

I like going to the IT room at school. It has about 40 really good computers in it and I sometimes spend my lunch times in there. They have a broadband connection to the internet and run Windows XP. I do my homework at lunch time and in class when they let me have a break. I really don't think that there should be any homework; instead there should be an extra hour or hour and a half of school. I think there should be a time for school and a time for home, and after you've done your six hours or so at school you shouldn't have to do another two hours of school work at home.

My family

I find it much easier to socialize with my family than with other people and I only ever feel really comfortable at home. We get along just like any other family really – sometimes I like them and sometimes I get annoyed with them. I do get angry with my nine-year-old brother Joseph quite a lot though. I know he's only nine and I shouldn't get so annoyed, and besides I should be used to it by now, but he just makes me so angry. He's got ADHD and he's really, really annoying. He just tries to annoy you in any way that he can. Yesterday he just came up to me and for no reason hit me in the teeth making my lip bleed. I had to really restrain myself from hitting him back. The other day we had a huge fight. We were doing Taekwondo and I accidentally hit him on the head with my elbow. It was a pretty light knock to the side of the head but it was enough to make him angry, and he started fighting and hit me really hard in the face. I was so angry because I had only hit him by accident. The problems between Joe and me have got worse lately. I think it's because Joe has been stealing food that's not gluten- and casein-free and he's reacted badly to the food. He's been an absolute pain. Mum thinks it's because I'm so obsessed with playing Runescape that I can't stand anyone distracting me away from the computer.

Mum and I clash about things just like any other teenager with his parents. Aside from the computer and my spending too much time on it, we clash because Mum is too fast for me. I'm a very slow thinker and it takes me a long time to do things. Mum will shout, 'Luke put your Taekwondo uniform on,' and by the time I've processed the information she's shouting in my ear again.

My future plans

I'm definitely planning to get an IT and Design GCSE and then maybe an A-level. I want to become a website designer and programmer in HTML and Javascript. I don't think I will go to university. I don't really see the need to as you can do HTML courses outside of university, and university life isn't all that appealing to me.

CHAPTER 7

Simon's Story

How do you make friends? I mean, you don't just go up to
someone on the street and say, 'Hey do you want to be my
friend?' No – that would be weird.

Simon was born in Perth, Australia, in 1989. Although his mother is Australian and his father American, Simon has never lived in those countries. He left Australia as a young child and has grown up as an 'expat' kid in Asia. He considers himself to be American and would love to live there one day. When we first met Simon and his family they were preparing their fifth international move, from Singapore, where they had lived for the past three years, to Indonesia. Simon had mixed feelings about this latest move. He would have preferred to move to America, a country that he both admires and has a fascination for, but felt happy that his dad, an accountant who had recently resigned his job, had found a new position in Indonesia. Simon had been unhappy in his small special education class at a British international school in Singapore, so one bonus of moving countries was that he was leaving the school he had disliked so much. His mother, Anne, feels that much of his disaffection with the school was due to his not wanting to be in the special education stream:

> He has trouble being identified with the kids he perceives as
> dumb kids with a lot worse disabilities than him. But Simon has
> learning difficulties on top of Asperger's, which is not always the
> case: normally Asperger's kids are very bright and can function
> well in the classroom, but their behavior is odd and their social
> interaction is odd. And I know a lot of AS kids that go to regular
> schools and manage. Simon does need help in the classroom.
> And because he needs help he's been put in a special education
> class with six kids and a teacher aide as well as the teacher who is
> special education trained. He doesn't feel comfortable in there.
> He doesn't want to be in there, he doesn't want to associate with
> those kids.

To date, Simon has always attended international schools and within this
context finding schools suitable to his needs has been a challenge for his
parents. He started primary school in Japan, where he attended a mainstream American international school. Unfortunately he never settled
into the school and his parents had to make the difficult decision to take
him out of mainstream schooling and place him in a special education
school.

> He was wandering off mentally and physically and couldn't
> focus on the class. Previously he had attended a Montessori
> program where he was able to move to different learning centers
> within the classroom as he wished. We were called in after the
> first month to tell us that he had problems, and we were in severe
> shock; it was a very difficult time for us adjusting to the severity
> of his issues that were bad enough that he couldn't stay at that
> school. We had no choice but to put him in a special education
> school, which was such a hard thing for us to come to terms
> with.

Both Simon and his mother are now anxious about finding the right
school for him in Indonesia.

Simon was born with cerebral palsy. Then at the age of seven he was
diagnosed as having an attention deficit disorder and started taking the
drug Ritalin, which he continues to take. Anne describes her feelings
about the ADD diagnosis:

We felt he had a lot of symptoms of ADD, non-attentive type, but there were a lot of symptoms that really didn't fit an ADD child. He had this extreme anxiety when he would get stuck on things. And he had a lot of behavioral issues, like he would get extremely anxious of walking into a place that had been re-carpeted. Why? If they changed the carpet he would notice these things, he found the change disconcerting and upsetting. His filtering system wasn't very good. He couldn't understand why things had changed. Or if you changed the way to walk home he would get terribly upset. He couldn't deal with walking on the opposite side of the street. 'No we should cross over here – we should go here – you shouldn't do that…'

Anne noticed that Simon played differently to other children. He pre-ferred solitary or parallel play, as children do at an early age, but unlike the other children Simon did not progress to social play. Even now Simon is a homebody who prefers his own company. He dislikes crowds and as a child would be difficult to take to shopping centers unless the trip was to *his* favorite shops, such as computer shops. Anne says:

He likes to isolate himself, so he spends all his time in his room. To get him to go out, you can bribe him and say, 'Every time you take the dog for a walk around the building I'll give you 50 cents.' He'll remember and do it twice in the week and then forget all about it. He's quite content with his own company.

At the age of 11 Simon was diagnosed with Asperger Syndrome. Anne had read Tony Attwood's book *Asperger's Syndrome* and felt she was on to something – so much of it seemed to fit what the family had been experi-encing. This prompted her to see another professional, this time an expert on Asperger Syndrome. Anne describes the process of coming to what she felt was the 'best fit' diagnosis:

We were reading the ADHD books and we decided that Simon had all the symptoms except that he wasn't hyperactive. So I followed up on ADHD and when we went to a behavioral spe-cialist he said, 'Well, he appears to have a lot of these symptoms but we are not going to place this label on him because it's really not like the hyperactivity-type ADD. Its more ADD not ADHD.'

ADD kind of fit but we felt there's more to it. So we can kind of say well he has cerebral palsy, he has ADD-type symptoms, he has learning disabilities, or if you say 'Asperger's' it almost fits all of the things which are going on. Not everything – but almost.

Anne has found that the diagnosis of Asperger Syndrome has been of enormous benefit. She feels that learning about Asperger Syndrome has allowed her to understand Simon and to help him learn the social skills he needs to form meaningful relationships with the people around him:

> When you have an understanding of Asperger Syndrome then you can do a lot more preparation for him in helping him understand what the world is all about. Like he needs to be made aware of things so he knows 'well if I do this then people might think that I'm a little bit odd. So maybe I should, you know, try to change that behavior just a little bit.' For example, I said to him, 'You walk in the house and you never say "Hi, Mum, I'm home!"' So tonight he did! He said, 'Hi, Mum! Where are you?' I said, 'I'm in the study.' 'Hi, Mum, I'm home. I've only got so many days at school left now until holidays,' and I said, 'Oh yeah, that's right.' And so it wasn't like him just storming into his room and closing his door. We actually had 30 seconds of social interaction because I prompted it. He doesn't understand that perhaps that's a nice thing to do, so you have to explain to him: 'This is something I quite like. People like that little social interaction even though it's a very short quick thing, people really like it.' So he has to learn some of the behaviors that we take for granted. Because I understand the label more and I've done a lot of reading, then I can help him as well as spending a huge amount of money on therapists.

When Simon first arrived in Singapore he was very unhappy and withdrawn. Moving to Singapore from his previous home in Japan was a difficult transition for him to make. He was subsequently diagnosed as clinically depressed and took the antidepressant medication Prozac for two years. Anne describes Simon's low self-esteem and the depression at this time:

> His low self-esteem was really evident, because if you are depressed you don't function very well in any aspect of life. You

want to isolate yourself – which he's really good at doing, isolating himself at school and in every situation: not wanting to go on family outings, not wanting to go on family holidays except when there's something specifically he's interested in. And we knew medication was the right thing for him – despite our reluctance – when he started smiling after a few doses.

Simon recently started attending a small social-skills training group for teenagers with AS run by an educational psychologist. His mother feels he has flourished in this group and that it has greatly improved his self-esteem and made him more receptive to social interaction:

> Over the last few months he's realized 'Oh, there are other kids just like me that go to other schools!' To meet up with other kids who have similar issues to deal with has been the best thing for him, because he doesn't feel that he's completely alone. It has done wonders for his self-esteem. He's happier, he's a lot more willing to have a conversation with you, as long as you don't interrupt him when he's doing his homework. He wants to do things as far as social interaction is concerned, but on his own terms, when he wants to.

Like most adolescents, Simon is exploring different possible identities. He has lived in Asia since he was 15 months old, and as a 'foreigner' or 'expat' wherever he lives this has posed all sorts of identity issues. He has recently begun to strongly identify himself as an American – an identification spurred by the destruction of the World Trade Center on 9/11 in New York and the talk at school about who would win the elections between Bush and Gore. He's passionately patriotic, and this new-found patriotism fuels an earlier almost obsessive interest in American presidents and American culture.

Simon has a seven-year-old brother Andrew, who was recently diagnosed with ADHD. The two brothers are often incompatible in many ways. Anne describes an example of this:

> Andrew's very demanding. And he's very social – he wants to be with someone all the time. Simon wants to be alone. That's the conflict. Simon wants quiet time. He needs downtime after

school. He needs to be on his own for a while and Andrew wants to be with someone at all times. That causes problems.

A great deal of Anne's time is spent catering to the needs of her two demanding boys. Andrew constantly seeks attention, is easily bored, and would love to play with Simon – but Simon spends a lot time trying to keep him away, out of his room, so that he can find the peace and quiet he so enjoys when he is playing computer games. Anne often has to play with Andrew because Simon wants to be left alone – and Andrew is an active playmate who easily flits from playing with a walkie-talkie, to playing with blocks, to wanting a drink or something to eat. He is very easily bored.

When we first met Simon his right leg was in plaster from a recent operation. As a result of his cerebral palsy Simon has had to have several operations over the years. The latest operation involved lengthening his Achilles tendon to allow him to walk comfortably. Simon copes well with the surgeries. Anne, a trained nurse, knows she needs to be on the lookout for physical signs of pain – sweating, fast pulse, restlessness – as Simon rarely articulates feelings of pain.

Simon lives on the sixth floor of a large and comfortable condominium in Singapore. He seems a little tall for his age, with short-cropped blond hair, large round brown eyes, and a clear complexion. Like most 13-year-old boys, he seems uncomfortable in his body; as if it's one size too big for him. He wears braces on his teeth and speaks in a slightly American accent. He has an expressive face with reasonably good eye contact. He also seems quite emotional. When we talk about his experiences with bullying he looks as though he might cry, and he looks quite fierce when he talks about retaliating against the boy next door who has been teasing him.

Simon finds it very difficult to articulate his thoughts and feelings. At times he seems about to burst when he wants to convey some feeling but the words seem to be frustratingly out of reach. Anne says:

> Sometimes when someone asks him a question and I'm in the room, he'll look at me and want me to answer. It's sometimes hard for him to give a response when you know there's a lot of thought processes going into what he might want to say. So if I'm in the room he'll look directly at me and want me to respond

to the question. And then if the person, say he is a psychologist, says, 'No, Simon, I'd like to hear what you would say,' he might shrug his shoulder or he might say three words rather than a detailed response. He's not sure how to get the words. He might have the feelings but he can't get the words.

In the time we spent together Simon preferred to talk in his bedroom away from his brother. We sat in his bedroom which is very comfortable and self-contained. Simon has his own computer, a large TV, and a video player. He spends a lot of time in his room.

Simon talks about his life

Asperger Syndrome and socializing: How do you make a friend?

Making friends is hard because the question is 'How do you make friends?' I mean, you can't just go up to someone in the street and say, 'Hey do you want to be my friend?' No – that would be weird. Then when you do talk to people it's hard to fit yourself into the conversation. I feel like that at school sometimes. Sometimes I'm sitting next to some kids and I might be able to say something, but not very often. I feel different from the kids in the other classes – you hear them talking about stuff but it's hard to get yourself into their conversation. They talk about normal kid stuff. I can never start a conversation like they do. I don't know where to begin making friends or what to say and how to start friendships.

I'm in a small class at school – there are only four students now. The other kids in my class are not that brainy and they do stupid things. Like this one other kid, he's autistic. I know that he's really nice and he can't help it, but sometimes he's an idiot. Then all the other kids in the school look down on our class, they call our class 'the class for silly kids.' I don't really want to be in this class at all – the other kids have worse problems than mine and I find it hard to talk to them. I'd much rather talk to adults anyway. One good thing though is that I'm the smartest in the class. That makes me feel good. But there are only four people in the classroom so it's quite easy to get to the top!

If there's one thing I could change that would be my relations with other people in the school. I don't have anyone that I hate but I would just like to get to know them more. I think the Asperger's blocks me from making friends. I've been told that it affects how social you are. I think the Asperger's is definitely a part of why I find it difficult to make friends. I do have one friend, though. I met him at this group for Asperger kids that I've just started going to. I really enjoy that group and I look forward to it every Friday. He's a really good friend to me and we get together in the weekends. We play computer games on my PC – our favorite game is Warcraft. He told me that in the latest Warcraft humans and orcs combine forces to fight the armies of the undead! He has Asperger's as well but he's just a little bit different from me. I mean, everyone has a different personality. There's something that he talks to me about, and I should really keep it secret and it does sound a bit silly, but he wants to dominate the world! He's going to use bugs, not computer bugs but insects! He wants to take control of them and just invade a country. I told him, 'Don't you dare attack my country because if you do you're going to war!'

The Asperger group has four kids, including me and this friend. There were five but one of them left because he's moved to Hong Kong. I couldn't believe it when I went to the group that there were all these different kids like me going to different schools. It made me feel good. We talk about things like having Asperger's. The good thing is I don't feel embarrassed with them because they also have it. I feel a lot more relaxed and happy with the Asperger group kids – it's easier, you know, because they have the same problems as me. During the group we learn about different problems, like last week we talked about moving countries. We've also talked about making friends, what to ask a friend when you meet them. I watch the time on Fridays because I don't want to be late for the group.

Being teased makes me feel angry. When I started school in Singapore a couple of years ago the kids teased me – I forget how. But there was a school psychologist and she managed to stop it. They don't know I'm different. They don't know about Asperger's. Recently my neighbor was teasing me. He's ten years old. He has this technique of teasing – it's just not something you can ignore. Like one time he had this chocolate and he knew I wanted some. He threw it in the toilet and then he asked me, 'Do you want some chocolate? Go and look in the bathroom.' I went into the bathroom and there it was in the toilet. I don't know why he would do that. I think maybe it's a part of growing up. I did try to scare him so he wouldn't mess with me. I kind of threatened him. I picked up a stick and I whacked it hard on the floor and said, 'If you don't stop teasing me then…that will be you.' He was like, 'Ooh I'm so scared.' He was faking it. So we don't get along at all. The chocolate thing started it.

I also had an enemy in my old school in Japan. I don't know what happened but one day he just said, 'I'll be your friend today, but tomorrow I'll be your enemy.' And the next thing you know he was my enemy! It's really weird because I have no idea what happened at all – I did nothing. And then all of a sudden he says this strange thing about being my enemy. Then he started teasing me and being mean. I don't know why he did that, because we used to get on pretty well before.

Computer games: Getting stuck on one thing

I'm good at computers. I've had my computer for about five years and it's still going. My favorite thing to do is to play computer games. I'd play those games all the time if I could. When I come home I like to go into my room and play computer games. I often have the TV on as well, tuned to CNN. If I have the TV off it feels like something is missing. I'd describe myself as obsessed with computer games. I just get stuck on one game and can play it over and over for hours. Mom says that I could play computer games 24 hours a day! My computer is my own and is only used by me. My brother has his own computer. If he came in and tried to use my computer then I'd get mad at him.

Once Mom came in and watched me play The Sims. She said my Sims were in a terrible state! They hadn't eaten or showered, the garbage hadn't been taken out and I had all these Sims sleeping on the floor. It was pretty hard keeping all the Sims going, making sure that they all got jobs so that they could buy beds and stuff. I also have this rally game where you drive through the streets of Chicago. I have a special steering wheel for that. Once I played this with Mom and she said, 'I'm not ever driving with you!' We were running into walls and crashing everywhere and she said, 'Oh my God!' and I said, 'Mom, it's only a game!' I play computer games with my friend from the Asperger group who comes over sometimes.

Schools, international schools, and feeling rejected

When I was five we moved to Japan from Indonesia. There are two American schools in Tokyo and I went to both of them. The first American school I went to – the school and me didn't get on. I remember Mr Miller, he was my teacher there. He was tall. I don't know what the heck happened but I left the school. They didn't say that I had Asperger's but I just wasn't learning anything there. I could only count to ten and that was it! I liked the second American school I went to in Japan. It was small, just a house, and I learnt to write there. There were only about 15 kids in the whole school. I have happy memories of this school. This was a special education school and I made friends with a Dutch boy who also has something similar to Asperger's. When I came here to Singapore things were harder. I've never really liked the school in Singapore. I haven't had many good times at this school. I'm in this special class with four other kids and I've got kind of a mean teacher. He's not the right kind of teacher for me – he's not the right kind for anyone. He uses the same punishment for everything. We have this homework book that we have to sign to show that we've done our homework. If we don't sign then he gives us a detention. Now, isn't that a bit much? I'm the only one who doesn't get detentions because I'm always good at behaving. But I feel bad for the other kids and I'm getting sick of it. I mean, they are getting so many detentions I'm like, 'This has got to stop.'

No one likes this teacher but I don't think he really cares. He says that there are people in the world who will hate you no matter what you do. And it's because he can ignore the fact that a lot of us don't like him that he dishes out so much punishment. If he minded what we thought of him he'd probably be a bit easier and wouldn't give so many punishments for silly things, because he wouldn't want people to hate him.

I remember one really bad time at my school in Singapore. It was a long time ago and I cried because of the PE teacher. He had a really bad temper and was always yelling. I was pretty scared of him. This one time I walked across the yard to get the right kind of baseball mitten as I had the wrong kind. I didn't know it but some kids and the PE teacher were already playing baseball in the yard that I was crossing! The PE teacher got really mad at me – he started shouting and even threw balls at me to get me out of the way. Once he started hitting me with the balls I just got really angry and started to cry, and I was thinking, 'He should get fired.' Then he picked up the bat and he started hitting more balls at me; he didn't aim for my face but he was like scaring me. I think that he was trying to teach me something the wrong way. But you should never scare kids to teach them. You should talk to the kid rather than just throwing a bunch of anger at them. But I couldn't say anything and all I did was just cry for the rest of the day. Then this other teacher came and took me to the art room. He was on my side, see. He just had me stay in the art room until I calmed down, and he wasn't angry at me or anything. I told my mom and I think that she talked to the principal. The teacher is still there but he's not the PE teacher anymore.

Sometimes I get very angry at school. But I don't like to talk about it with anyone. I don't like to discuss those feelings – they are very private for me and I like to keep those things to myself. I'll only tell Mom if I think it's really ridiculous. Now we're getting ready to move to Jakarta and I'm quite upset about the international schools there as I've already been rejected by two American schools and by one British school. I think that all international schools should be controlled by the country they represent and not by the country they are in. In the USA and Australia it is against the law to reject kids. I wish that law would be used all around the world then it wouldn't be such a problem. I told my mom that I would like to contact the United Nations and tell them about it, but she said that it wouldn't do any good. I also know some friends who have the same problem as me.

Asperger Syndrome and identity

I found out I had Asperger Syndrome about a year or two ago. I went to see this doctor in Australia who was an Asperger's expert. It was kind of strange how he tested me because what he did was show me pictures and then ask, 'What's missing in this picture?' Now how does that actually prove that you have Asperger's? I think AS does describe me pretty well but I like to keep it quiet. I don't want anyone knowing that I have a syndrome or anything. I don't want people at school to know at all. It would be too embarrassing because then they'll know that I'm different from them. The only kids I've told are the kids in my class. It's okay to tell them because they also have something too. I think one of them probably has ADHD like my brother Andrew. I'm not sure, but he does have something.

What is Asperger Syndrome? Well, it's not contagious! I was born with it and it affects how social you are. I do think it's a little bit of a disability because it holds me back socially. There are also obsessions on stuff, getting stuck on one thing, like with me it's the computer and computer games. That's why I feel much more relaxed and happy being in the group with the other kids with Asperger's. They have the same problems as me. I think the Asperger's will affect me less in the future because in some people it doesn't affect them after they are adults as they get better control of themselves.

My family

I have a brother Andrew who is seven years old. I remember the first time I saw him in the hospital and he was crying. The nurse picked me up to show him and he had a big red face! We had two different rooms at first, but when the maid came she got Andrew's room and I had to share with Andrew. We had bunk beds and I was at the top. I remember once I put him on the top bunk and when he woke up he didn't know how to get down. I did the same thing again but this time Mom and Dad came in and put Andrew on the bottom bunk. They put me on the top while I was asleep. One time we both slept at the top.

My brother is a little devil. He's always up to mischief. He has ADHD and he's very hyperactive. He just can't be alone. He's completely the opposite of me. We don't really do things together. We just have separate lives, different lives. I get really angry when my brother refuses to go out of my room. And it happens quite often. I just want to play my computer games on my own and he comes in and he's not allowed. I usually have to get Mom to come in and get him out. First of all I tell him to go out, but he usually refuses. It's quite funny because he actually begs! He gets down on his knees or bends down and says, 'Please let me stay, please.' I told him that begging is not going to work because otherwise he'll think that by begging he can stay in and you know then I'll have to give way all the time. So it's better to just say 'No.' I do love him though, because he's my brother. But I'm not very good at telling him that.

My dad's an accountant. He travels around quite a bit for his work. He had to get a new job because he resigned from his old one – it was a very large company and everyone resigned from the firm because of something that happened back in the US. A while ago my dad decided that we'd do one family thing a week, and we'd all have to join in. But it wore out after a while, until my brother remembered it again and then we started doing it again. We don't really do stuff like go out and eat at McDonald's very often. What we'll usually do is someone will go out in the car and go get it and bring it here and we'll all eat here. I can't really remember the last time that we all went out together. Usually we'd just do something at home.

My future plans

I don't really like to discuss my future plans. It's very private and I want to keep it all to myself. It does involve my interests in politics and computing, and that's all I can say about it at the moment.

CHAPTER 8

Themes and Issues from the Stories

The life stories of Lee, Rachel, Sarah, Chee Kiong, Luke, and Simon give us an insider's view of the experience of growing up with Asperger Syndrome. During the course of our discussions with the teenagers and their families many important topics and issues were raised that help us to better understand the childhood and adolescent experiences of someone with Asperger Syndrome. In this section, we focus on the following six key themes that emerged across the stories and discuss these in relationship to other research on AS:

- diagnosis as a sense-making narrative
- labeling and identity
- socializing and making friends
- the dilemma of schooling
- family life
- rages and the blues.

While we found that the teenagers shared many common experiences, we want to avoid generalizing from their stories and make claims that this is necessarily what life is like for a teenager with AS. Luke commented on a tendency in the literature to present sweeping statements about 'people with AS,' as if purely by virtue of having the label 'AS' these individuals now form a singular homogeneous group, or as Luke describes them 'Asperger's clones.' We have chosen to focus in depth on a small number of teenagers and to examine, as much as possible, their unique circumstances and individual experiences of growing up with AS. In fact all the teens we spoke to are complex and unique individuals: they are first and foremost Lee, Rachel, Sarah, Chee Kiong, Luke, and Simon, and not simply representatives of AS. Obviously, sharing a label in common brings with it many shared characteristics and experiences, whether due to common traits or the way society views and treats you, and there was plenty of evidence of this across the stories. However, we also found that while AS had clearly shaped these teenagers' perceptions of themselves it certainly didn't subsume all other aspects of their identities.

Diagnosis as a sense-making narrative

A common thread across all the stories is how the diagnosis of Asperger Syndrome provided the families with an explanation for their child's unusual behavior. All of the teenagers we spoke with shared an unusual early childhood: for example, often they were late talkers or were dyspraxic or clumsy, had routine behaviors or were very rigid about certain things, and exhibited a focused and unusual fascination with certain subjects or objects (Luke's early love of batteries and pencils, Sarah's passionate interest in animals). The formal diagnosis of AS provides a story or an explanation for these peculiarities. In other words, AS becomes a sense-making narrative that provides a framework for both the child and the family to understand an often confusing and frustrating early childhood. For all the teenagers, AS became an integral part of their life story and self-identity; it explains why they sometimes feel different from other kids and why their early childhoods are different from those of many of their peers. A common reaction to first hearing the diagnosis is a feeling of what Lee called 'pure relief'; here at last is an explanation for why certain situations are so difficult, why it is so hard to talk to people, or why it is so hard to get organized before school in the mornings. Chee Kiong recalled that 'even before I had heard of Asperger Syndrome I knew that people thought I was different in some way.' Diagnosis involves learning about AS and reevaluating one's own life story as one's early childhood and current problems are interpreted in light of not only medical 'diagnostic criteria' but a wealth of other narratives about AS that are read – in the growing body of Asperger literature – or swapped as reminiscences in special classes, support groups, listservs, or egroups.

The teenagers we interviewed generally support Clare Sainsbury's (2000) recommendation that children be told their diagnosis as early as possible so as to reduce their own confusion and feelings of personal failure. For many kids, diagnosis brings a sense of relief: *'I'm not stupid, or crazy, I have Asperger Syndrome!'* Luke, for example, was annoyed when he discovered that his mother had known for years that he had AS, as the diagnosis allowed an alternative and more positive self-image to the one that he had been holding on to over the years that he was 'just clumsy and stupid.' Initial reactions to the diagnosis do not suggest that teens feel that they are being labeled or placed in a group, rather AS provides an essential explanation for why they find it hard to make friends or to handle social situations. In Simon's words, 'I think the Asperger's is definitely a part of why I find it difficult to make friends.' Learning about AS allows them to reflect on their own behaviors and cognitive processes; they can now identify certain types of 'AS thinking,' such as getting stuck on a particular task or topic, as well as numerous sensory sensitivities. Although parents may feel apprehensive about telling their child about AS, the life stories indicate that the value of the diagnosis lies in its power to make sense of what many children have experienced as 'years of social confusion' (Howlin 2003).

One initial reaction to diagnosis is shock and disbelief. Luke, for example, said: 'It all felt a bit unreal and I wanted it to be proven to me somehow with medical tests or something.' Chee Kiong remembered that he had 'mixed feelings' on hearing his diagnosis: 'The reason why I felt really confused is that I wasn't sure whether I was *really* different from normal people. But then I realized that autistic people are almost the same as normal people – it's just that they can't socialize.' The recognition of his social difficulties meant that he accepted AS as an explanation for his problems and his difference from others. Although some felt shocked at first and, in Luke's words, 'wanted it to be proven to me somehow with medical tests,' no one we interviewed disagreed with their diagnosis. In fact most of the teenagers felt that the diagnostic criteria aptly described their characteristics. For example, Sarah said: 'My mum first talked to me about Asperger's. She was talking about Bill Gates having it, and that got me interested. And then she said that maybe I have it and she started describing things about it, and most of the things she described are what I have – it's so strange!' Like the others, Sarah totally accepted the diagnosis and did not consider alternative explanations for her differences. This acceptance may simply reflect the widespread attitude that medical diagnoses are infallible truths.

In some instances there was also a degree of fuzziness in terms of the diagnostic criteria and which diagnosis provided the 'best fit' explanation. This was definitely the case for Sarah and her family who are still confused over Sarah's earlier diagnosis of ADHD and the more recent one of AS. In this instance, therefore, the diagnosis of AS has reduced value as a sense-making narrative. Sarah's parents struggle to deal with two competing models for understanding her behavior: Does she have ADHD or does she have AS? Sarah's mother Catherine said: 'Now, how I deal with a tantrum depends on which way I look at it. Do I deal with it by calming her down or do I reason with her, by trying to explain? That's our dilemma.' Although the family are very close, there is a polite disagreement over Sarah's condition – Catherine believes that Sarah 'has got both AS and ADHD,' but Peter, Sarah's father, isn't sure about the diagnosis of AS. Sarah, however, accepts that she has both ADHD and AS: 'When I found out that I had Asperger's I knew why I couldn't have friends that easily, why I liked to make strange noises, and why I was so interested in animals.' The shifting sands of many diagnostic categories does little to help matters.

Labeling and identity

Developing a self-identity involves an individual making conscious choices about the attributes and traits he or she incorporates into this identity. Identity is never fixed but is woven in the narratives we tell others about who we are. A key issue facing each adolescent is the degree to which they identify with the diagnosis of AS and define themselves according to this label. In each life story we see differences between the characteristics used by the person to describe himself or herself and the perceived attributes of people with Asperger Syndrome as a social group. Writing a life story involves a careful consideration of the individual's reflections on self-identity: Who am I and how should I describe myself to others? However, we are not so free to mold our social identities or how others perceive us.

How people with AS are seen as a social group depends in part on popular conceptions and misconceptions of that group. In the 1970s 'people with autism' were seen as severely disabled people with little hope of living normal lives and were rarely represented in popular culture (Shore 2003). In the 1980s and 1990s, films such as *Rain Man* and *Mercury Rising* portrayed the autist as a savant hopelessly lacking all but the most rudimentary ability to communicate with others but nevertheless endowed with exceptional computational skills. In the early 21st century, representations of autism and AS are undergoing rapid change: the savant still dominates popular thinking, but there's also a growing recognition that people with an autism spectrum disorder may include highly successful people such as Bill Gates and Albert Einstein – even if these people have never claimed to belong to this group.

In the process of forming a self-identity we were interested in exploring how the teenagers situated themselves in relation to their AS. How does the knowledge that they have AS factor in to how they see themselves and relate to others? What is it like to be placed in a group and be told that you suffer from a social learning disorder? How does the teenager deal with the diagnosis and label of AS? As we interviewed the families, we felt that each teenager, in the process of forming an identity, must deal with at least five fundamental issues raised by the diagnosis. We've put these issues in the form of questions because we believe that these questions, although rarely explicitly posed, must be somehow addressed by the adolescent:

- Do I accept the diagnosis as valid or do I seek another explanation?

- Do I consider AS a disability?

- Which parts of my self-identity and my thinking are due to my AS and which parts are just me?

- Who do I tell about my AS?

- How do I deal with people's assumptions about AS?

Do I accept the diagnosis as valid or do I seek another explanation?

Not one of the teenagers we interviewed felt that he or she had been misdiagnosed. Given that we asked for volunteers to help with our research, we expected this acceptance as it would be somewhat odd to agree to help with our book only to declare that you did not in fact believe that you had Asperger's. As noted in the previous section, many people feel a great sense of relief on hearing their diagnosis as it provides an explanation for many of their difficulties. It is also worth noting that at present the medical explanation for the behaviors that comprise Asperger Syndrome dominates the AS literature and remains largely uncontested. Furthermore, on an individual level most people see medical diagnostic categories such as Asperger Syndrome as scientifically established truths rather than social constructions open to re-interpretation.

Do I consider AS a disability?

Only two of the six teenagers, Simon and Chee Kiong, felt that AS was a disability and that by virtue of this fact they were disabled, particularly in the area of social relations. None of the others had incorporated the notion of disability within their identities and some even championed the strengths associated with AS, such as greater concentration and high abilities in some areas. Luke, for example, saw himself as having the positive end of the deal in the tradeoff between the strengths and deficits associated with AS. Lee was skeptical of the notion of AS being a disability, arguing that our perceptions of disability are to a great extent subjective:

> I wouldn't term Asperger Syndrome a disability. One way of looking at Asperger Syndrome versus neuro-typical-ness is that everyone else (NTs) has a gift for emotional or social under-standing but they've got this disability in abstract concepts. It all depends on your viewpoint.

While these teens did not see themselves as being disabled, they did see themselves as being 'different' from 'normal kids' and had all needed to somehow incorporate this notion of 'difference' into their sense of identity. Our interviews suggest a relationship between self-esteem and the extent that the teenager views AS as a disability. Chee Kiong believes AS to be a lifelong disability with zero benefits: 'You can't take it away. If I could change myself and get rid of the Asperger Syndrome then I defi-nitely would.' His view of AS is tied to his frustration at not being able to make friends, his shyness, his difficulties in judging appropriate behavior in social situations, his reluctance to think about dating; in short, his low self-esteem. He doesn't see any connection between AS and the areas where he does excel: his diligent study habits and drive to do well at exams, his abilities in mathematics, his powers of concentration, and his aspiration to become a cardiologist. Simon, who has learning difficulties, also sees AS as a barrier to social interaction and nothing more: 'I think the Asperger's blocks me from making friends.' One response to a diagno-sis of AS is to identify it as the source of all one's difficulties in making friends; an entirely reasonable response given the diagnostic criteria of the DSM-IV.

As noted above, most of the adolescents did not view AS from an entirely deficit perspective. While they may accept the downside of AS – such as difficulties in making friends and understanding social interac-tions – without claiming savant skills, they also acknowledge that, in Luke's words, 'the good points of having AS outweigh the bad.' For Luke, his powers of concentration more than compensate for sensory issues and social difficulties. The intellectual joy afforded by an absorption in a par-ticular subject or problem can be seen as one of the unsung gifts of being on the autism spectrum. To acknowledge these gifts is to begin to see AS as a double-sided coin: the DSM-IV only describes the 'tails' side whereas the 'heads' side is only beginning to be described in the growing body of Asperger literature. Surprisingly, the 'heads' side of AS nearly always involves a love of machines and systems, especially computing, and there is ample anecdotal evidence that children on the autism spectrum display a proficiency in this area far beyond their neuro-typical peers (Blume 1997; Singer 1999b). For Rachel, the 'heads' side lies in exceptional intelligence as, like Lee, she describes her intelligence as being inextricably entwined with her different way of thinking: 'If I could change myself and get rid of Asperger's, I honestly don't think I would because I'm sure I'd lose part of my intelligence.'

These differences raise the question of whether or not AS should be considered a disability. As we have noted earlier, Simon Baron-Cohen (2000), an experimental psychologist at Cambridge University and noted researcher in the autism field, argues that there is nothing in the neurobiology, behavior, or cognitive style of people with AS that can be identified as a disability; rather, AS should be understood as a neurological difference. While children with AS are often fixated on objects and things rather than interested in people this does not mean that they are disabled: 'For example, a child with AS/HFA [high-functioning autism] who prefers to stay in the classroom poring over encyclopedias and rock collections during break time, when other children are outside playing together, could simply be seen as different, not disabled' (Baron-Cohen 2000, p.491). Chee Kiong might spend his lunch time studying for his exams but that doesn't make his activity any less valuable than his classmates.

While many of our adolescents would agree with Baron-Cohen that they are different rather than disabled, all accept that they experience some difficulties at present and have experienced profound difficulties in the past that have required support, attention, extra resources, and understanding. For our families in England, a formal diagnosis of autism was essential for getting access to services and support from local education authorities. Lee said: 'I saw the diagnosis essentially in terms of the benefits it could provide me, such as access to a good school where everyone could understand me and I could do my best. I never saw it as a "label" in the negative sense of the word.' Rachel's mother Helen also sees benefits in the label: '…to me, even though there's a lot of controversy about labeling, there's a lot to be said for it as long as the facilities are there and you can access them.' In terms of self-identity, adolescents may feel more positive about the label AS and not see it as a stigma if they can identify benefits they have received from that label such as the provision of special education or, as in Sarah's case, membership in an Asperger teen social group. Chee Kiong, who was, in our view, least happy with the label, did not see any benefits whatsoever from being identified as having AS. His perspective needs to be contextualized within his Singaporean Chinese cultural background, which places great value on conformity. It is understandable then that Chee Kiong would have a negative attitude towards the diagnosis of AS as he clearly feels that it is the AS that sets him apart and prevents him from conforming to social expectations. Furthermore, for Chee Kiong within his cultural frame of reference the label carries with it a definite stigma.

Which parts of my self-identity and my thinking are due to my AS and which parts are just me?

Adolescents diagnosed with AS face an unusual challenge in forming their self-identities: they must sort out for themselves which aspects of their own personalities, interests, and behaviors display AS traits and which aspects have nothing to do with AS. Nita Jackson, a teenager diagnosed with Asperger Syndrome and bipolar affective disorder, puts it this way:

> I'm confused about the world and its mainstream majority. What would it be like being mainstream? Would I even have these problems if I were a mainstreamer? Would I still be so confused? Is Asperger's Syndrome as bad an affliction as I make out? (N. Jackson 2002, p.49)

Parents also wonder what aspects of their teenagers' lives are due to AS and which are typical features of adolescence with all its challenges.

For a moment, imagine yourself as a teenager with AS. There is a growing body of literature on your 'syndrome' that lists all the common features of the AS personality. You recognize some of these features and a feel a wave of relief that you're not crazy, nor are you alone! But wait a moment. Is your huge interest in astronomy due to your Asperger's, or is it just that you've always loved outer space and learning how the universe works? What about your ability in computing, or your ability to remember, in detail, pictures, photographs, and CD covers – even if you are terrible at remembering the names of some of your classmates? Is that all part of the AS too – or do 'normal' people also have their own little peculiarities, interests, and quirks? Thinking about Asperger Syndrome requires you to think about your own thinking, about your hobbies and interests, not to mention how you sense and perceive the world. Adolescents often put themselves under the microscope and can be highly critical of their own quirks, seeing each as a flaw. For the AS teen, each flaw is dutifully observed and documented in Asperger literature. The danger in over-identifying with AS lies in it becoming a black hole which would engulf all aspects of your personality and life: you would only see yourself through the looking glass of your syndrome. You wouldn't *have* AS – you would *become* it.

For Rachel, the need to develop a sense of her self-identity outside of her AS was identified by her art therapist. Rachel's art therapy encouraged her to explore other aspects of her personality and to look beyond the label to identify traits that were an integral part of her rather than mere symptoms. Rachel feels that this therapy allowed her to recognize that she has more in common with neuro-typical people than differences and that she's first and foremost *Rachel* rather than 'Rachel: the girl with AS.' Luke acknowledges that he finds it 'quite difficult to distinguish which bits of my personality are AS traits and which bits are just me.' His strategy is to closely watch 'NTs,' all the while paying attention to how their behavior differs from his own. Luke has worked hard in his books, radio shows, and public talks to stress that all people with AS are different and are not to be treated as 'clones.'

While Lee accepts that he finds some social situations difficult to understand, he no longer identifies with the AS label, simply seeing himself as a computer scientist. Lee was the oldest teen we interviewed and is an example of how thinking about one's identity changes over time and with maturity. Theorists in developmental psychology, such as Erik Erikson (1968), have argued that the primary developmental task of adolescence is forming a cohesive identity or addressing the question 'Who am I?' During this process of identity formation the adolescent experiments with different identities and attempts to piece together the various elements, both conferred and constructed, that uniquely define him or her. During late adolescence, when the teen is grappling with additional and more complex elements of identity, such as a vocational identity, a political identity, a religious identity, and so on, it is likely that his or her sense of identity will be less heavily based on earlier, simpler, and perhaps conferred, aspects of identity. For adolescents such as Lee and Rachel who have experienced a marked decrease in their AS 'symptoms' as they have grown, their present sense of identity is clearly less dominated by their diagnosis of AS. AS simply holds less significance in defining who they now are.

Who do I tell about my AS?

When a person tells another that he or she has Asperger Syndrome, they come out of the neurological closet and reveal part of their self-identity to another. In doing so, they now present their AS to others as part of their social identity. This carries with it the risk of being stigmatized and viewed only in terms of stereotypes of the group to which they belong. Disclosure presents a particular dilemma because, in Stephen Shore's words, 'the person on the higher end of the autism spectrum must often contend with being somewhere between the visible and invisible type of disability' (Shore 2003, p.287). Unlike a physical disability, AS could *almost* pass unnoticed, allowing disclosure to be avoided. If the person is moving through the autism spectrum as they mature, then he or she may have greater freedom not to disclose as the visible signs and peculiar behaviors fall away. But what does one do when one can spend all one's energies, in Willey's (1999) phrase, 'pretending to be normal' but at the cost of masking all one's frustrations, anxieties, and interests? And how does one deal with the numerous misunderstandings of autism? Parents have often told us variations of the familiar denial response, usually uttered by Granddad, or sometimes by a school teacher: 'She can't be autistic, she can talk! And she's looking at me!' There's always the possibility that a person may refuse to believe that a child has Asperger Syndrome, a refusal that often betrays the listener's dogmatic views on what counts as autism, or a belief that parents are jumping on an 'autism' bandwagon, or that kids are just naughty and need discipline. What if you tell and they don't believe you?

While for most teenagers we interviewed the primary difficulties lay in problems with understanding social situations and making friends, rather than being labeled, disclosure was nevertheless an issue that they each needed to address. Do I decide not to hide that I have this condition called AS – which doesn't mean that I have to shout it from the rooftops – or do I only tell a few people, or do I keep it completely hidden? One factor in making this decision is whether the teen attends a special education school or class. Disclosure carries less risk within a special education school and can almost be a casual exchange of information, as we see in Rachel's account of how, when she was seven, she ran around the playground telling everyone 'I've got Asperger Syndrome' only to get a 'Yeah, whatever' response. Lee's experience in the Chinnor Unit was somewhat similar in that while the kids in the mainstream school to which the unit was attached looked at the kids from the Unit 'as freaks,' the closed environment within the Unit allowed him to become friends with other kids there 'having the same kind of support.' In both cases the special education environment places kids in a group where the stigma of being identified as having AS is practically eliminated and disclosure carries fewer risks. Simon doesn't 'want people at school to know at all' that he has AS, even though he does think that 'AS does describe [him] pretty well,' but he has told the kids in his special education class as 'it's okay to tell them because they also have something too.' The popularity amongst the adolescents for Asperger support groups and autism support-related activities all indicate that such groups take away the pressure of 'pretending to be normal.'

What remains unclear to us is the extent to which stigmatization plays a role in the social difficulties experienced by a child with AS. Why is it, we wonder, given that AS, as a medical syndrome, is characterized by a child exhibiting poor social skills and the inability to make friends, that when that child is placed in a less hostile environment with other children there is frequently a marked increase in social interaction, and friendships often develop? The ability to form these friendships in safer environments may indicate that stigmatization, or at least the child's sense that they are different from others, might be a factor in preferring solitary play, although other issues, such as sensory overload, may be important as well. At present we know surprisingly little about how AS adolescents form and maintain friendships (Gutstein 2003).

The extent to which a person discloses to another person or group of people determines the degree to which AS becomes part of their social identity as opposed to being just a part of their self-identity. As a published author and AS advocate, Luke is the most open about his AS. In part, his openness came from his desire to tell others about the benefits of the GF/CF diet as well as frustration at the misconceptions and generalizations that people have about AS. Luke says that his disclosure hasn't made much difference to him because most of his peers remain ignorant of AS. When a BBC film crew came to shoot footage of Luke at school for the documentary *My Family and Autism*, Luke did notice that he suddenly became incredibly popular and that the whole school wanted to talk to him in front of the camera (L. Jackson 2003). Obviously, Luke's work, along with the work of authors such as Clare Sainsbury, Nita Jackson, and Kenneth Hall, goes beyond mere personal disclosure and seeks to change and improve the social identity of adolescents with AS.

Many teens may choose not to disclose, especially if they are moving through the spectrum and feel that many of the major difficulties they have faced are passing with time. Lee informed the university in his application form that he has Asperger Syndrome, and he still helps with autism support activities, but he prefers not to tell other students. He sees no advantage in disclosure and believes the information would only complicate his new friendships at university – although he may need to disclose in the future to a long-term partner. Chee Kiong finds any disclosure painful as he worries that malicious classmates would use this information to spread rumors about him around the school. He also worries about the lack of understanding of autism in Singaporean society: 'They think that autistic people are hopeless cases, that they are mentally abnormal people who can't be changed or saved, which is just not true.' Although Chee Kiong knows about a social support group for teenagers at the local Autism Resource Centre, he feels that such a group would distract him from his studies and that his AS is a problem best left for him to deal with alone. We feel that his fear of disclosure and being stigmatized should be understood in terms of the lack of general public awareness of autism in

Singapore, which does not have the degree of special support services and media coverage of disability issues found in the United Kingdom.

How do I deal with people's assumptions about AS?

As we mentioned earlier, the assumption that all people with autism have savant skills can be directly attributed to the lack of imagination of Hollywood script writers. There are two types of assumptions: the assumptions held by people who know next to nothing about autism and Asperger Syndrome and whose knowledge is limited to *Rain Man* and, at the other end of the assumption spectrum, the assumptions of those who may be all too familiar with the medical literature. Both Lee and Chee Kiong mentioned misconceptions about savant abilities. Luke also mentioned the problems of AS people being seen as a homogeneous group:

> We are always a group, you know, like clones. We get generalized a lot: AS people are like this; this is what AS people do. You have to fit a certain description. For example, you have to have difficulties making friends, look down at the floor all of the time, wave your hands in the air, and so on. It's like every symptom has to be ticked off.

The preconceptions Luke has to deal with clearly don't originate from popular films. For Luke, the danger of the label lies in people who are familiar with the DSM-IV diagnostic criteria and the growing literature on AS expecting adolescents with AS to display every symptom. We know how difficult it can be after a diagnosis not to see that person's behavior or interests as a symptom. Every behavior – from being bored at a party to loving Sonic the Hedgehog – can be viewed with a scrutiny few 'normal' children would ever be subjected to and duly noted as yet another AS trait. Some of these traits are in our view clearly wrong. For example, the common belief that adolescents with AS don't enjoy fiction or fantasy literature was rejected by nearly all of our teens, many of whom took great delight in fantasy literature, especially Terry Pratchett's *Discworld* series. In an ironic twist, Luke quipped to us, that a love of Terry Pratchett is so widespread amongst AS teens that it 'could be used in the diagnostic criteria!'

Socializing and making friends

The increasing importance of friendships is a major feature of adolescence. Typically an adolescent may spend almost a third of their day in the company of their friends; more time than any other age group (Gutstein 2003). Tony Attwood (1998) suggests that it is during adolescence that people with AS start to become more interested in socializing with others and wanting to fit in and make friends. Often at this time their difficulties in this area start to come into sharp relief and can lead to depression and other emotional problems. Certainly the biggest stumbling block for most of the teenagers we spoke with was being able to make friends. Chee Kiong in particular felt that his lack of friends, which he directly attributed to having Asperger Syndrome, was by far the greatest problem in his life. He had thought about the situation long and hard and pragmatically came to the conclusion that he desperately needed friends:

> The worst problem for me in my life is socializing. I cannot make friends and I need friends badly. When you have friends you get more support and you can ask a lot of things from them and they'll help because they're your friends. You also gain a lot of knowledge and experience from your friends. And because I don't have friends it means that I'm cut off from help. Whenever I have a problem I have to handle it on my own. I don't know how to socialize and that means I don't know how to use people to my advantage. To me that is the biggest problem with having Asperger Syndrome.

This perspective is in contrast with Luke's view (L. Jackson 2002) that, like him, most people with Asperger's are quite happy with their own company and do not particularly want to socialize. Luke in fact urges parents and teachers not to be too 'pushy' and force their kids to socialize:

> I don't mind my own company at all and have nothing in common with most other boys. This seems to cause teachers a problem. One teacher told me it was time I stopped being a 'Billy No Mates' and got out there and started having fun. As if his idea of fun was the only way – yeah right! That actually upset

me and frustrated me quite a lot. Being alone doesn't. I would say that if you don't want to mix with people and are quite happy on your own, then carry on and don't let anyone push you into anything different. (p.165)

It is difficult to validate the perspective that perhaps people with Asperger's simply do not want to socialize and that being on their own does not cause them undue distress. In our group of teenagers, particularly amongst the boys who were in their early teens, unhappiness over social isolation and loneliness was a common theme in our conversations, suggesting that friendships *were* considered important. Even Luke spoke of his feelings of loneliness and frustration with his lack of 'social instinct.' Sarah's mother Catherine described Sarah's need for friendships as so desperate that she often overwhelmed her friends with her need:

> She wants her friends 100 per cent of the time. She wants them to not have any other friends. In the past she'd come home from school and want to ring them up straightaway. She'd want to have sleepovers together. It's like nothing was ever enough.

Psychological research would suggest that, while friendships may not be necessary for survival, they certainly enhance any human being's emotional and physical health and quality of life. During adolescence, when teenagers are spreading their wings and gradually moving away from the protection of and dependency on parents, the need for friendships will be even more underscored. Amongst the three boys, Chee Kiong, Luke, and Simon, the lack of social engagement was very apparent. None of these boys socialized regularly. Simon's main regular social activity was attending a weekly social skills class with a small group of other AS teens and meeting up with one of the boys from this group to play computer games. Luke told us that the last party he had been to was two years ago.

In his discussion of AS teens and friendships, Steven Gutstein (2003) cites a study of teens with high-functioning autism and AS that suggests that these teens lack a real understanding of the emotional value of friendships, seeing friends as playmates rather than as sources of emotional support. In our group of teens, with the exception of Simon who found it extremely difficult to articulate his views on friendships, we found that the desire for real friendships, based on emotional bonds, was very strong. Chee Kiong in particular desperately wanted what he described as a 'sincere friend' who could provide him with much-needed emotional support. In their definitions of what makes a person a friend the teens seemed to value loyalty and the absence of ulterior motives for the friendship above all else. For example:

> To me, a good friend is someone who doesn't lie and who isn't insincere or dishonest. It is someone who shares things, their interests – not just knowledge or how to do homework. (Chee Kiong)

> I think a good friend is someone who is loyal and doesn't talk about you behind your back. It is someone who is understanding and a shoulder to cry on. A good friend is someone who is fun and a nice person and with whom you share some things in common, but not necessarily everything. (Rachel)

> A good friend is someone nice who you can trust and who doesn't tell you to do stuff like 'Go and do this for me and I'll give you money' or something. (Sarah)

In other words a friend is someone who likes you for who you are and who will stand by you. We felt that the teens we spoke with broadly understood the nature of friendships, and how friendships can provide emotional support, but often experienced immense difficulties in being able to make and sustain such friendships.

Experience sharing

The question then arises how friendship skills can and should be taught. In his essay on AS teens and friendships, Steven Gutstein (2003) describes a mode of interaction called 'Experience Sharing' that he suggests is fundamental to forming friendships. He further argues that the key deficit of Asperger Syndrome is the lack of relative information processing skills for Experience Sharing. Experience Sharing involves interacting with others specifically to share ideas, feelings, and perceptions; allowing us to create deeper emotional bonds with others; for example just chatting with a friend on the phone about nothing in particular and for no apparent purpose. Experience Sharing involves thinking about and perceiving the social environment in relative rather than absolute terms. An example of 'relative' thinking in the context of social relationships would be 'Is my conversation topic interesting enough?; whereas an example of 'absolute' thinking would be 'I must always look at someone when they are speaking to me' (Gutstein 2003, p.110). In many social-skills programs for AS children and teens there is a tendency to focus only on teaching 'absolute' formulas for behaving in specific situations. As such these programs only go part way towards helping AS teens develop the skills necessary for forming and maintaining friendships. Having the motivation for Experience Sharing is a prerequisite for working to maintain friendships. Gutstein (2003) suggests that unlike other teens, AS teens, with their divergent social development and experience, have probably missed out on hours of experimenting with and mastery of the skills necessary for Experience Sharing:

> In effect, they develop their own unique brand of 'social science' that excludes the study and mastery of reciprocal, Experience Sharing relationships. The teenager with AS may continue to actively pursue social interactions throughout his life. However, by never entering the arena of Experience Sharing, he misses out on the most challenging and exciting and rewarding aspect of the social world. Without the motivation for Experience Sharing, the youngster never spends the thousands of hours and conducts the extensive personal research and self-discovery process by which typical children become such experts at relationship building and maintenance. (p.112)

In our group of teenagers the lack of interest in and exposure to Experience Sharing relationships is clearly evident amongst some of the teens. Luke, for example, described how he could never really understand the need to 'hang out' with friends or chat with friends on the telephone like his teenage sister:

> My sister once asked me, 'Who do you hang around with?' and I was like, 'What do you mean hang around with?' It took me ages to figure out what 'hang around' means, but I now know it's all a part of being social, like speaking with people on the phone and going to clubs, and so on. I don't hang around with anyone really. The downside is that I do get a bit lonely, but most of the

time I see no reason to hang around in these big wolf packs. And I've never seen any reason to just speak to people on the phone unless I've got something specific to speak to them about. My sister can chat away for hours on the phone with her friends. She's like, 'Oh my god, oh, he didn't! He did? No!' It's just like those American sitcoms. I find it utterly stupid, to be honest.

Similarly with Chee Kiong, classmates at secondary school would contact him frequently, but not out of friendship, rather to solicit information about academic work and homework. Of all the teens in our group Rachel was the most socially successful with a few close reciprocal friendships. Rachel clearly relied on her best friend for emotional support and shared her innermost feelings and experiences with her. Steven Gutstein's work provides a valuable framework for understanding the friendships of AS teens; he has developed programs for teenagers based on teaching Experience Sharing and friendship skills.

The pressure to conform

In talking about his social difficulties, Luke identified his conversational skills, which tend towards steering most social conversations to his favorite topic of computing, as being irritating for others and a barrier to making friendships. Similarly, Chee Kiong and Simon both spoke about how difficult they found it to know what to talk about with other teenagers, to establish common ground, and 'fit into their conversations.' Chee Kiong had turned this frustration into anger and was very derisive about his peers at junior college and their interests – Why on earth should he be like the others and talk about things that hold no interest for him like mobile phone models, even if it's trendy? The quandary then for some of the teenagers is whether to embrace their uniqueness or try to fit in by adopting some of the same interests and attitudes of their peers. Liane Holliday Willey (2003), in an essay reflecting on her teen years as a person with AS, also describes this sense of not really understanding her peers. Rather than reacting with derision, however, Willey chose to fit in by simply imitating the reactions and actions of her friends:

> I distinctly remember how hard it was to pretend to understand the various rituals and rites of passage that my peers seemed to

> enjoy when we were all teens. I knew enough to copy the actions of the few people I could trust. My formula was simple enough. When one of the friends I trusted laughed, I laughed. When they cried, my eyes welled up. When they expressed anger, so did I. (p.180)

Many AS teens, then, have to make the hard choice as to how much they will mask their real personalities and adapt themselves to group standards in order to gain social acceptance. Many of the teenagers we spoke to had not conformed to the standards of their peer group, or they had tried to conform but hadn't managed to get it quite right. These teens did not have social acceptance. They lacked credibility with their peers and were seen as being odd or uncool.

The question of whether it is better to conform or not to conform is a difficult one to answer. On a superficial level, conformity can take the form of imitating popular fashions and interests. As discussed earlier, it can simply involve learning absolute formulas for social behaviors, such as how to dress. In *Freaks, Geeks and Asperger Syndrome* Luke Jackson (2002) offers advice for those AS teens who want to adopt this strategy:

> If you really do want to blend in a bit more then you could make yourself look 'cool'. Get a new haircut, dress in trendy gear (easy to know what that is – just look out for designer labels...ouch – expensive!). This is fine and no problem, as long as you like it and are comfortable in it. Never make yourself feel uncomfortable for the sake of fitting in. (p.166)

Nita Jackson (2002) speaks of her experiences as an AS teen and argues that conforming may not always be the answer:

> I've tried to conform, with little success. Conforming didn't make me any more normal and has only ever given me grief. After years of fighting a losing battle, I eventually opted for the alternative rather than the conventional, which is the only way I could arrive at an acceptance of myself. Conformity is not the right way for everyone and this is nothing to be ashamed of. I've learned that with a number of Asperger people, trying to be someone you're not is impossible... So the only solution, I believe, is not to conform. (p.16)

While social acceptance is important, often allowing the teenager to keep 'under the radar' and perhaps not stand out as such an obvious target for bullies, Gutstein (2003) makes the essential point that, while it may be a prerequisite, obtaining social acceptance is *not* the same thing as forming and maintaining a real reciprocal friendship. A further problem is that attempting to mold yourself into something you are not, to fit other people's expectations, can ultimately lead to feelings of low self-esteem: 'People will only like me if I pretend to be somebody else.'

The dating game

Dating and sexuality were topics that the teenagers we interviewed were reluctant to talk about. Tony Attwood (1998) suggests that among AS teens a strong attachment to or sexual interest in someone occurs later than usual. None of the teens we spoke with were dating, and the three older teens in the group, Lee, Rachel, and Chee Kiong, definitely expressed their intention to defer looking for a girlfriend/boyfriend until they were older:

> In general I feel that girlfriends at university are a waste of time. You're at university to study and I think it's a huge distraction. I'm sure the people with girlfriends don't do all their work. (Lee)

> I'm not really interested in having a boyfriend. Not many of my friends are really that boy mad or have boyfriends either. Sometimes I do think about it but not very often. I wonder how I can be friends with a boy before he becomes my boyfriend because I read somewhere that all the best relationships start out as friendships. But I guess I find it easier being friends with girls than boys at the moment. (Rachel)

> I think that I should be conservative and wait until I'm older, once I get a job and am more stable, before I start to date. Maybe then I can find a partner that I can trust. There's no point just simply looking for some beautiful girl to say 'I love you' to and then later on getting a divorce. I *know* that I'm the type of person who doesn't take risks, so I'll wait until I'm older. (Chee Kiong)

Although the teens intended to wait before dating, this isn't to say there was no sexual interest expressed at all. Rachel and Sarah, for example, both spoke of having crushes on boys. The oldest teen in our group, Lee, had experienced two intense internet relationships with girls and had been planning to physically meet Marie, his French-Canadian internet girlfriend who lives in Montreal, before their online relationship ended. He describes the relationship with Marie as close and emotional:

> My first girlfriend was Marie who is French-Canadian and lived in Montreal. We used to talk every night via a net meeting. Obviously it wasn't a physical relationship and we didn't go out, but it was emotional. We saw each other via webcam and we formed quite a close relationship.

While Lee never directly acknowledged so, indirectly he indicated that he sometimes found it difficult to establish appropriate boundaries in his relationships with girlfriends. For example when his first internet girlfriend started becoming more distant and eventually confessed that she'd met someone else Lee hacked into the new boyfriend's computer and 'discovered some rather incriminating photos of him and her together.'

Some of the teens stoically acknowledged that their general social difficulties would also translate into difficulties in the area of dating and that's why they weren't trying to get dates. For example, Luke said:

> At school there's a lot of talk about who's going out with whom and people flirting with each other, but getting a girlfriend isn't really a high priority for me at the moment. I can't say that it preys on my mind – I've never really followed the crowd and thought I must do this because everyone else is doing it. I think it's stupid to be different to everyone else just for the sake of being different, but then again it's also stupid to try to fit a specific social status. I also don't think it's an issue as I doubt any girl would actually go out with me anyway. I just don't think I'm boyfriend material.

Similarly Chee Kiong stated:

> I'm not dating at the moment. The girls know that I'm not as charming as the other boys. They find me very lonely and very

quiet – very individualistic. I think they think of me as a typical Singaporean male who is very uncool and lacking in sexual appeal. Because they don't have a good impression of me, there's no reason to ask them out for dates.

In Chee Kiong's case it is worth mentioning the cultural context of Singapore which also plays a role in his attitude. There is a common perception in Singapore that Singaporean males are serious, unromantic, and inept at dating. The large and increasing numbers of both male and female professionals who remain single has even prompted the Singapore government to establish a government agency, the Social Development Unit, which attempts to 'match-make' single professionals and even produces guides to teach dating skills.

Self-esteem and achievement

Of all the teenagers we spoke with, Lee projected the greatest self-confidence and self-esteem. Although Lee had never attempted to conform to group expectations and had never achieved social acceptance, he had somehow managed to come through his difficult social experiences still feeling good about himself. A few explanations can be offered for this. Lee had experienced considerable academic success, and these successes could be counter-poised against the negative social experiences. Lee's high IQ (he proudly told us his genius-level score of 142) and academic accomplishments already set him apart from his peers, but not in the inferior position of a child with a disability, rather in the superior position of a gifted student. Lee himself framed his social difficulties as being the result of his giftedness: he was bored and unchallenged by the school curriculum and misunderstood by his peers at school who were not his intellectual equals. For Lee, clearly the issue is one of intelligence:

> All this petty teasing and bullying is just part of the ethos of some people. These are the people who just don't want to be at school. They're certainly not there to learn. I'm sure you'd very rarely see someone exceptionally intelligent going around bullying autistic children. I noticed the change in my sixth-form year at school. A lot of the bullying that happens during GCSEs just disappears. All of a sudden everyone has a common focus

because you don't do sixth-form unless you have a real interest in your subjects. Everyone else just drops out to go work in Waitrose.

In this way perhaps Lee was able to deflect the experiences of bullying and rejection away from himself and place the onus on the perpetrators. This is very difficult to do for those teens who have a more fragile sense of self-worth and do not have obvious talents or achievements to bolster their self-esteem. Another crucial factor that helped Lee was that his talents in mathematics and computing were shared and nurtured by his parents. Unchallenged in these areas at school, Lee was extended at home by his parents, who are also academically accomplished, and under his father's guidance he studied higher-level mathematics and computer pro-gramming at a young age. Lee's sense of pride in his abilities then was fostered young and enabled him to put a 'positive spin' on his differences from other kids and his difficulties. Similarly for Rachel, her high IQ, her Mensa membership, and her creative talents are used by her and her mother to counteract any 'deficit' perceptions of her due to her Asperger's. Her mother Helen describes the motivation to have Rachel join Mensa:

> I thought it would be really valuable because her primary school had been brilliant. When she first went in there she was a screaming wretch, and through all that they recognized the academic ability in her. I wanted to make sure that no other school or academic placement was going to be unable to recognize that. We could always say, 'Yes she has difficulties but she is a member of Mensa so don't labor under the misapprehension that she is not bright!'

For Lee, unlike some of the other teens we spoke to, social success is less critical to his feelings of self-worth. He is very focused and driven by his work:

> My focus at Oxford is definitely my work, although I do socialize. I certainly wouldn't say I was the most sociable of people and I'm not going to win any popularity contest in my college, but I do have a group of good friends. I don't feel isolated at all.

Friendship and special schools

A question that interested us was whether the teenagers we spoke with found it easier to socialize with other 'Aspies' than with 'neuro-typicals'; a related question being whether special schools are a more conducive environment for AS teens to make friends than mainstream schools. Of all the teens in our group Rachel had experienced the greatest success socially, having established close reciprocal friendships and a school life free from teasing and bullying. Both Rachel and her mother are clear that attending good special schools has contributed to Rachel's social success. One of the obvious benefits of special schooling is small class sizes allowing greater opportunity for the kids to get to know one another and for the teacher to create and sustain more positive social interactions in the group. Another positive attribute of special schools mentioned by Rachel is the absence of any stigma attached to being 'different.' At Rachel's school all the kids are 'different' in some respect and so the differences are in effect cancelled out. Sarah and Simon made similar points when talking about their social-skills group for Asperger teens:

> The thing that I really like about the group is seeing people who are like me – other kids who have these big interests. James is funny. He never smiles except if you say 'a giant insect' or something. He just has a frown on his face like all the time and we're like 'Hello! Smile!' It's just so good to feel normal. At school I have to control myself sometimes but in the group I can just be normal, just be myself. (Sarah)

> I couldn't believe it when I went to the group that there were all these different kids like me going to different schools. It made me feel good. We talk about things like having Asperger's. The good thing is I don't feel embarrassed with them because they also have it. I feel a lot more relaxed and happy with the Asperger group kids – it's easier, you know, because they have the same problems as me. (Simon)

Being in a special environment also eliminates the need for any dissembling about the label. Rachel notes that at her school everyone is very casual and open about their 'special needs.' It is definitely not a source of embarrassment:

My friends know I have Asperger's and one of my friends has got it too. Before she came into my class in Year 10 she visited the school for a few days and we got along really well. One day when we were out on a school trip I was just chatting to her and she asked me what special needs I had. I told her I had Asperger's and she said, 'Oh me too!'

In contrast, Chee Kiong, who has always attended mainstream schools, sees his diagnosis as deeply private and confidential and that disclosing the information to his school mates would be socially disastrous for him:

I don't like to tell people that I have Asperger Syndrome. It's a personal thing. It's very confidential because I know that people at school are very gossipy and if I were to tell them about my personal problems they would start to spread rumors about me.

Similarly Sarah, who attends mainstream school, is secretive about her Asperger's after having a bad experience when she was open with a friend about her ADHD:

I told one friend I had ADHD because I needed to go to the school nurse to get my pills and she had to come with me. Later when she wasn't my friend anymore she told the whole school. So it's like the whole school knows now! And she made it sound like a disease that's catching. One friend even emailed me saying, 'You're just not my type. You're not the kind of friend who I'd hang around with.'

It is important to note that the special schools that Lee and Rachel attended were very supportive of their needs as Asperger teens. Lee's school was specifically designed for teens on the autism spectrum and he was able to establish some friendships there with other teens who shared his passion for computer programming. Some special schools or classrooms are clearly not suitable for 'Aspies,' as Simon experienced in Singapore. Being in this class only served to weaken Simon's self-esteem and socially isolate him.

The dilemma of schooling

How best to survive the schooling system is a dilemma faced by many families with an Asperger's child and is another common theme in our teenagers' stories. Luke's mother Jacqui Jackson notes that surviving mainstream school is probably the most difficult hurdle faced by kids with AS:

> If you've made it through school then you're over the worst. You'll never enter a job where people are charging around corridors and knocking each other over and that kind of stuff. If you can make it through school then you've done the worst of everything!

From reading many personal accounts in the AS literature and speaking with teenagers with AS it is clearly evident that schools, with their general inflexibility towards what will be learned, when it will be learned, and how it will be learned, coupled with all the complex social skills required to safely and successfully navigate through them, pose a huge problem for many kids with Asperger's. The old cliché of square pegs and round holes often does seem apt. In general, the social dimension of schooling rather than the academic, posed the greatest difficulty for the teens. Apart from Simon, who also had some learning difficulties and needed academic support, most of the teens in our group were academically above-average students, a few of them exceptionally so.

The outsiders

In our conversations with the teenagers attending mainstream schools it was apparent that most of them did not feel a sense of belonging at school; they were by and large outsiders, outcasts, and deemed to be uncool. In Chee Kiong's words:

> My classmates look down on me. They look down on people who are not so trendy. They think of me as mature and outdated. I talk about things they don't like. They talk about hand-phone models – so called fashionable things, but I don't see why fashion is so important.

Similarly Luke talks about his relationship with Matt, a school friend:

> We both like talking about computers and things. But he's trying really hard to fit in with the popular crowd and because I'm considered to be uncool he said we can only be friends outside of school. He thinks his reputation would be ruined if the other kids saw him talking to me.

This perception of being uncool definitely marginalized these teenagers. And in fact all of the teenagers we spoke to, with the exception of Rachel, seemed either unaware of or uninterested in typical teenage 'cool' pursuits and interests. Rachel was the one exception who spoke of 'trendy' alternative music and music videos, fashion, and current cult TV programs popular with teenagers such as *The Osbournes*. Not surprisingly, of all the teens we spoke to, Rachel seemed to have least difficulty in making friends. For Rachel, having the 'right' interests made it easier for her to fit in with her peer group and make friends; conversely, having friends probably helped her to keep her finger on the pulse of teenage trends. For some of the more socially isolated teenagers, such as Luke, Chee Kiong, and Simon, having less access to information about current fads and trends and what is cool, which teenagers commonly share amongst their friends, probably contributed to their 'uncoolness' and lack of social acceptance at school.

In Lee's case, rather than a lack of credibility in the 'cool' stakes, it was his aggressive retaliation against bullying that put him well beyond the margins of acceptability by both his teachers and other students:

> A lot of the aggression at school was retaliation against the kids picking on me. I would attempt to give back as good as I got. I would always have the last punch, as you'd say. The other kids enjoyed getting a reaction out of me, winding me up, like: 'Let's go and spit at Lee he might do something amusing like smash a window' …most likely with one of their heads!

This cycle of bullying and aggressive retaliation effectively isolated Lee at school, and at times he was not even permitted to interact with the other children, being kept in the classroom or library at recess and lunch times.

Bullying and marginalization

We found from our conversations with the teenagers that bullying, teasing, and marginalization at school were, without exception, common experiences shared by all of those who attended mainstream schools. In Luke's case the bullying was so severe that following one particularly ugly incident he was left with no choice but to change schools. In his new private school the bullying has lessened but he is still socially isolated. For Lee, bullying and aggression at school have been a constant issue, beginning in preschool and resulting in his eventual exclusion from two local primary schools. For Chee Kiong in Singapore, being a 'social outcast,' as he describes it, has been ongoing throughout his schooling. Academic success is highly prized in Singapore society, by teachers, parents, and students alike, so Chee Kiong's studiousness and good grades have no doubt earned him some grudging respect from other students, and in the past students have approached him for academic information, but he has always been shunned socially. Sarah also spoke of incidents of bullying and teasing throughout her schooling, more recently in the form of internet bullying. In her present circumstances, with three good friends to support her, the impact of the bullying is probably buffered to some extent. In contrast to the others, Rachel, who has never attended mainstream schools, told us that she has never been bullied or badly teased. Rachel said that social difficulties with peers at school usually manifested themselves in situations where she has been the aggressor:

> Being teased has never been a problem for me, and in all honesty it's more often me that's being the bully. When I was in primary school there were these kids that I decided that I didn't like and I was quite horrible to them.

Mainstream or specialized schooling?

For many families then, given appropriate options, an uneasy choice often emerges between mainstream or specialized schooling. While home schooling is another option, it has limited viability for most families, including those we spoke to, due to the immense financial strain it places on families and the difficulties of finding suitable home tutors.

We feel that the question of whether to mainstream or not, with pros and cons on both sides of the argument, can only be resolved on an individual basis, being dependent on so many different factors: the resources and options available, the child's wishes and the extent of the social difficulties being experienced, changing government policies regarding provision for special education, and so on. The families we spoke to expressed a range of views over the question of whether to mainstream or not.

Lee's parents felt that he was on a road to disaster and that his considerable academic talents would have been left untapped had he continued in mainstream schooling. Lee himself stressed that being placed in a specialist school was the catalyst that turned his life around. Being out of mainstream school gave him a 'breather' from the terrible cycle of bullying, aggressive retaliation, and ostracism that had dominated his experience of schools up to that time. Freed up from the social pressures and in a small sheltered environment he was able to develop his interests in mathematics and computing. Without this respite and the flexible and unorthodox teaching methods adopted by school staff (e.g. initially Lee was given free rein to pursue his own interests at his own pace and not held to a strict curriculum) Lee may not have developed his talents and made it to Oxford. Lee's case clearly highlights some of the benefits of a specialist, protected environment.

Similarly, Helen, Rachel's mother, is a strong advocate for specialist schooling and feels that her decision not to mainstream has greatly benefited Rachel. For example class sizes at Rachel's current school are considerably smaller (her Year 10 class comprises only six students) than would be the case in a mainstream setting. Helen also praises the atmosphere of social acceptance promoted at Rachel's school:

> Her school is for girls of average and above intelligence but who would be vulnerable in a mainstream school. So there are some Aspies there. Her best friend is there because she has facial disfigurement. So they're all very accepting of people as people rather than as syndromes. It's actually a delicious, delightful school – just wonderful. It's like an Enid Blyton book. It's a big Victorian building with acres of grounds.

Helen feels that parents may no longer have the range of choices that she had when choosing schools for her children if the new push towards inclusion in the UK government's education policy, which she feels is only fiscally driven, holds sway:

> My LEA [local education authority] is making a big deal at the moment about inclusion and how the wishes of the parents are paramount. I said, 'Okay, if a parent of a special needs child wants the child to go to mainstream then their wishes are paramount, absolutely, but if a parent wants their child to go to a specialist school are their needs still paramount? No.' So it's very fiscally driven and they pretend otherwise. I know from contact with many chairs, governors, and other heads that mainstream schools don't feel they are the appropriate place for children with special needs because of a lack of training, resources, and money. There is also the big ethos of the league tables [school rankings]. Who's going to want special needs kids to bring them down in the league tables?

This quote from Helen nicely illustrates the complexities of educational choice within the harsh realities of the interplay between politics, economics, and educational policy. For some families then, depending on where they live and the government policies of the day, the choice to mainstream or not may be illusory.

Jacqui Jackson, Luke's mother, spoke of some of the problems of finding appropriate special schooling for Luke in the region of the UK where they live and the academic restrictions inherent in such schooling:

> It's a really strange set up in a way. We have a school for profound and multiple learning difficulties, a moderate learning difficulties school, and mainstream. That's it. Nothing exists that is specifically geared towards kids with Asperger's where you can also do all your GCSEs. Luke's always liked the idea of going to a special school but not if it means being restricted to doing only a limited number of GCSEs.

Jacqui also feels that a potential problem with special schooling is social isolation and that protecting AS kids from the harsh realities of life in a 'neuro-typical' world is not necessarily the best approach:

> Even if there was a school where all the curriculum was geared towards kids with AS and you could do all your GCSEs, it would

still be very isolating. The moment you're out of school there are all these typical, normal people waiting to chomp at your ankles, figuratively speaking, and you're not prepared.

The stigma of being in a special needs environment was a problem shared with us by Simon and his mother. Simon's mother, Anne, says:

> He has trouble being identified with the kids he perceives as dumb kids with a lot worse disabilities than him. But Simon has learning difficulties on top of Asperger's, which is not always the case: normally Asperger's kids are very bright and can function well in the classroom, but their behavior is odd and their social interaction is odd. And I know a lot of AS kids that go to regular schools and manage. Simon does need help in the classroom. And because he needs help he's been put in a special education class with six kids and a teacher aide as well as the teacher who is special education trained. He doesn't feel comfortable in there. He doesn't want to be in there, he doesn't want to associate with those kids.

In Simon's situation as an 'expat' in Singapore very few options for appropriate schooling are available. In general, most international schools in Singapore are not welcoming of children with special needs of any description. Similarly, in Indonesia, Simon was rejected by two international schools on the basis of his special needs. As largely private institutions, international schools are not mandated by any government policies to mainstream, and as such offer very little in the way of resources or programs for including special needs children in their classes. These schools are governed by the market, and from a 'cost-benefit' perspective they see little financial gain in being inclusive of special needs children who form only a small slice of the market. Having said this, some schools will *provisionally* enroll special needs children, but it is a sink-or-swim situation for these children as they are forced to mold and adapt to the school's requirements with no give or take being offered on the school's part to accommodate the children's needs.

Within this context then, Simon was enrolled in one of the few international schools in Singapore that promotes itself as having provision for special needs children. Unfortunately, as Simon's mother expressed to us, this school had little specialist expertise in Asperger Syndrome and tended to group all their special needs children, ranging from mild to severe, in one class, and, despite promises, offered very little integration into the mainstream program.

Third Culture Kids

As the children of foreign expatriates living in Singapore, Sarah and Simon can be considered to be 'third-culture' children. The term 'Third Culture Kids' (TCKs) was coined by two social scientists, John and Ruth Useem, who propose that expatriates often form a unique lifestyle and culture which differs from both that at home as well as the host culture. TCKs, then, are expatriate kids who, despite coming from diverse countries, nevertheless have shared experiences and characteristics. Being a TCK involves coping with an enormous amount of change and a loss of relationships. Both Sarah and Simon found the process of transition involved in moving countries extremely difficult. For Simon, moving to Singapore from Japan triggered a serious bout of depression. Sarah's mother, in describing Sarah's reaction to their move from Holland to Singapore, likened the transition to a period of intense grieving.

Schools are especially important for TCKs in forming social relations, as these kids are different from local kids. Most international schools, however, are characterized by constant student and staff turnover further reinforcing the transitional nature of being a TCK. Laura Cockburn (2002), an educational psychologist who has worked with many TCKs, argues:

> ...it is important for international schools to recognize the transitional *culture* within the school and understand that this requires special accommodations...and there is an enhanced need to focus upon social networks and the development of social skill supports within and outside of the school since schools form an important part of the student's social community that is difficult to provide elsewhere within the expatriate world. (p.484)

It is this ability to be flexible and adaptive to transition as TCKs that is most likely to pose difficulties for the AS teenager. For example, a hard-won friendship can suddenly be ended with either friend's return to their home country, only to have to start over again the difficult task of establishing social relationships.

As we discussed earlier, within the international school context children with 'special educational needs' are especially vulnerable, in that most international schools are reluctant to admit them and rarely provide resources for them. Consequently many TCKs with special needs are placed in inappropriate educational settings that fail to support them to their fullest potential (Cockburn 2002). This was clearly an issue for Simon and his family in Singapore and also in their subsequent move to Indonesia. Finally, as Laura Cockburn states in regard to international schools: 'One hopes that the "plight" of the student with special educational needs will improve. Currently a lack of awareness and a lack of regulation protecting and supporting such students and families cause great distress' (p.484).

Family life

Most of the teenagers we spoke to, even when prompted, did not want to speak at length about their relationships with their families. They eagerly shared information about school issues and friendships, but family seemed to be a less favored topic in our conversations with them. A number of possible explanations for this can be offered. Firstly, they may have felt that the topic was especially confidential. Secondly, many of the teenagers' parents asked to be present during the interviews, making it difficult for the teenager to then openly discuss family relationships. Thirdly, many of the teens seemed close to their parents and other family members and therefore did not feel the need to discuss the topic, preferring instead to talk about the more problematic issues troubling them.

Even amongst our small group of families we found a range of family types. Two of the families were single parent (Rachel and Luke), and in each instance the father had left the family when the teenager was a young child. Rachel currently sees her father regularly, but in Luke's case there has been no contact at all. All of the teenagers had at least one sibling with the two-child family being the most common. Both Lee and Luke came from larger families with three and five siblings respectively.

Our finding that in most of the teenagers' families another family member had also been diagnosed with an autistic spectrum disorder or ADHD, or a parent or grandparent displayed AS traits, suggests a genetic explanation for Asperger Syndrome.

Relationships with siblings

Many teenagers with AS have some particular difficulties in playing, socializing, and generally 'getting on' with their siblings. Some teenagers talked openly and frankly about how they got on with their brothers and sisters, while others, such as Lee, didn't readily offer much information. When looking at sibling relationships, a useful distinction can be made between what Luke's mother, Jacqui Jackson, has called a 'mixed house-hold' (J. Jackson 2003), where at least one child has ASD or ADHD and one does not, and an 'ASD-ADHD only household,' containing a teenager with AS and a sibling with either an ASD or ADHD. Our reason for including ADHD in the family equation is that two of the teenagers we interviewed had a sibling diagnosed with ADHD.

The difference between a mixed household and an ASD-ADHD only household is the presence of a 'neuro-typical' (NT) sibling. This NT sibling may remind the ASD child of his or her differences. As Luke reports, even though they are a close family, it's hardly uncommon for him to hear one of his sisters exclaiming, 'Luke, you are such a geek!' If the siblings are sociable, then, as Jacqui Jackson notes, this may only serve to remind the teenager with AS of the difficulties they face handling social situations and making friends (J. Jackson 2003). Luke can see how he's different from some of his sisters – they chat on the phone for hours and enjoy hanging around with their friends, whereas he doesn't 'hang around with anyone really' and sometimes feels lonely. If the downside of having an NT sibling is feeling different, the benefit is that the AS teen can see how other teenagers do socialize and, if so inclined, can go to a brother or sister for advice on making friends, asking someone out for a date, or personal problems. In some circumstances, the relationships between NT and ASD siblings can become strained, as NT siblings may feel that they are subjected to more scrutiny and higher expectations from their parent than their AS sibling (Stanton 2003). This can lead to feelings of resentment.

If a sibling has ADHD, then this can be a strain on the family. In Simon's case, he has AS whilst his brother has ADHD. Siblings with ASD and ADHD are often like oil and water. Simon likes to be alone with his computer, but his brother Andrew wants to play nearly all the time and finds it difficult to keep himself amused. Their mother Anne finds herself taking the role of a surrogate sibling, playing with Andrew to keep him happy because Simon refuses to do so. In a similar fashion, Luke sometimes finds it difficult to get along with Joseph, his nine-year old ADHD brother, whom he sees as often annoying him for no good reason, although he acknowledges that his mum believes that Joseph is seeking attention and trying to draw Luke away from his computer game. The ADHD sibling seeks attention and wants to interact and play, whilst the AS brother or sister prefers solitary play. We also suspect that in many families there is an ongoing battle over the amount of time the AS teen spends at the computer versus the time the family would actually like to spend with him. In contrast, a sibling with ADHD often demands attention and craves almost constant social interaction. In contrast to the AS teen, the family may often wish that the kid with ADHD would go and play on the computer by themselves just a little more often!

If a sibling or siblings have an ASD then birth order and the nature and degree of the ASD are paramount. Rachel expressed mixed feelings towards her elder brother James, who is 'full-blown' autistic and boards during the week at a special school. When they were children, James often engaged in challenging, difficult behavior that upset and frightened her. Part of her maturity in being able to talk about these feelings comes from the work she has done in therapy to recognize the way her own fears of autism and disability tainted how she saw James. Rachel's mother Helen appreciated the need for Rachel to work through these feelings so as to help her establish a sense of identity outside of autism and to move beyond relating to her brother in terms of her own fears of becoming 'like him.'

If the parents of an undiagnosed ASD child are unsure about the child's development, then the arrival of a non-ASD sibling and a comparison of their development over the next few years can prompt the family into a diagnosis of the first born. For example, the arrival of Lee's sister when he was two years old threw his unique developmental pattern into relief for his parents. Conversely, if the first born is diagnosed as having an ASD then this can lead to the parent being more attuned to the signs of autism in all its myriad variations and observant of younger siblings. Often this can lead to earlier diagnosis of younger siblings.

Family relationships as a whole

As we mentioned in our section on diagnosis, AS transforms family dynamics on a variety of levels. Parents often go through what Rebecca Moyes (2003) calls 'stages of adjustment' after hearing the diagnosis. They may find that the diagnosis profoundly transforms their relationship as they go through feelings of doubt, despair, anger, fear, and sometimes a 'mourning' for their own expectations of their ideal child (J. Jackson 2003). Living with a child with AS is often stressful, which can place a strain on the parents' relationship. Anecdotal stories from support groups suggest that the process of coming to terms with the realities of living with an AS child places a strain on the parents' relationship – fathers, in particular, are prone to leaving the family.

Contrary to the stereotype of adolescents with Asperger Syndrome being complete loners, both Chee Kiong and Sarah are obviously very close to their brothers. Chee Kiong shares with his brother a love of Japanese anime and movies – they often sit and talk about these interests. Sarah loves to play with her younger brother Andrew, who looks up to her and joins in with her fantasy play games. Their mother, Catherine, felt that Sarah and Andrew were closer to each other than most brothers and sisters. Although Luke didn't say much about his sisters, there's no question that the Jacksons are a supportive, close-knit family. While some adolescents with AS may not like being touched and may not willingly volunteer their feelings to others, we didn't find them all to be aloof or distant from their family. In fact, we found a number of close relationships: Chee Kiong expressed how close he felt to his mum and brother; Sarah and her brother Andrew are close; Rachel and her mum seemed more like best friends than mother and daughter and Luke and Jacqui have a great rapport with one another.

Family outings are more difficult for families with an ASD child, so there are often fewer family outings and visits to family friends than in other families. In a household with more than one ASD child there is more potential for family outings to turn to pandemonium as various siblings 'spark each other off,' a phenomenon Jacqui Jackson calls the 'domino effect' – her account of taking her family to the cinema is both hilarious and harrowing (J. Jackson 2003). The Jacksons had not been to the cinema as a family since the birth of five-year-old Ben, who has autism. So Jacqui decided that a family outing with all the children – Matthew, Rachel, Sarah, Luke, Joe (who has ADHD), and Ben was a good idea. She carefully ensured that she brought everything she needed to help Ben in the bright, noisy cinema (large coat, comfort goggles, nappies, dummy, cup, change of clothes, special sweets). She was able to avoid the long queue and stopped to ask about the ingredients of the popcorn and mints, as the boys were on a gluten- and casein-free diet, only to see the girls skulk off to buy their own sweets. Of course, Joe wanted to eat the girls' chocolate, and in his rush to get the sweets spilt his popcorn all over the floor. From then on things fell apart. There was no way that Jacqui could manage to pick up the pieces, so she decided it was best that they return home. Jacqui writes a lucid account of how simple family outings often require the detailed planning (equipment, timing, logistics) of a SWAT team mission. The parent must be constantly vigilant, almost on an adrenaline high, as she surveys and assesses each situation: Are the lights too bright? Is it too noisy? Is my child showing signs of distress? Is an incident or meltdown likely to occur? Family outings also mean dealing with strangers who may often peer down their noses and give disapproving looks as if to say *can't you control your child?* These strains frequently subvert the very aims of the outing – to relax, have fun, and chill-out together.

All members of the family must learn to ride the stormy waves of a tantrum or meltdown. Tantrums place a strain on family relationships, especially if the child is violent. Many children with Asperger Syndrome 'lash out' from an early age at members of their family when they are frustrated or when there are over-stimulated by bright lights, loud noises, or crowds of people. Family members are often wary of the volatile side of the AS adolescent, especially if that adolescent is becoming more violent as they enter puberty and hormones rage through their systems. The adolescent may slap, punch, or throw objects at members of the family – they may also become hysterical and try to run out of the house – as we saw in

Sarah's story – or they may direct this anger and frustration at themselves and bite or in some other way hurt themselves. Many people with AS tend towards being perfectionists, so for them there is often something embarrassing and distressing about these meltdowns. One reason, we suspect, that Lee was so reluctant to discuss his tempestuous relations with his siblings is that it would tarnish our impression of him as a young, academically successful computer scientist.

It's often a lot easier for the immediate family to recognize and understand the warning signs of an imminent meltdown. Other family members – such as grandparents – may be less familiar with and understanding of tantrums, or may respond to these tantrums by raising their voices or losing their tempers. At times the family's explanation for the meltdown may differ from that offered by the teenager. Many families feel that the teenager has to hold it together all day at school, making the most dangerous time of the day the first hour or so when they return home. Sunday evenings can also be a difficult time as the teenager faces the week ahead. These behaviors aren't limited to adolescents with AS: we all know adults who take their frustrations out at home after a hard day at work. While the family may attribute these meltdowns to stress, the teenager sometimes has another explanation. Chee Kiong's brother says that if Chee Kiong has had a rough time at school then any little incident may act as a trigger for a flaming row. Chee Kiong sees the matter differently: he can't bear to be contradicted, and sometimes any form of disagreement throws him into a rage, regardless of whether he's had a good or bad day at school.

We noticed that the teenagers – such as Sarah and Lee – who recognized the signs that they are under stress felt more confident that they were moving away from having meltdowns and had developed their own strategies for calming themselves down. Their comments support Tony Attwood's point that 'cognitive restructuring' can play a key role in managing stress: the aim of cognitive restructuring is not merely to manage stress by 'counting to ten' or taking a deep breath but to allow the person to recognize that they may have 'distorted conceptualizations' or may be responding to a situation in an inappropriate manner (Attwood 2003). Lee knows that he was right about the U-key incident: he had the IT skills to present the university café with the diagnostic specification and error code to prove that he'd been wrongly charged for his sandwich. But Lee also recognizes that the time spent proving that point and the rigid need to be right demonstrates a type of 'AS thinking.' This self-reflection allows him to keep a certain perspective on his own responses and actions and accept that certain responses may appear to others to be inappropriate. This self-knowledge and sense of perspective has greatly reduced his frustration in social situations.

Rages and the blues

According to Tony Attwood, current research indicates that 65 per cent of adolescents with Asperger Syndrome have an affective disorder that includes anxiety disorders, depression, delusional disorders, and conduct disorders (Attwood 2003). Many adolescents with AS may experience difficulties recognizing emotional states in themselves and in others (Howlin 2003). Furthermore, research also suggests a higher incidence of mood disorders in the families of children with autism and AS (Attwood 2003). There are various explanations for the higher incidence of these mood disorders, such as a genetic predisposition and possible differences in the composition of the amygdala, a region of the brain associated with emotions, as well as environmental influences and stress (Attwood 2003).

In talking with us, the adolescents did discuss two very strong emotions: anger, when they had tantrums, and feelings of depression. We've called these 'rages and the blues,' but we know that clinical depression – especially teenage depression, which along with teen suicides is rising alarmingly in many countries – far exceeds just 'feeling blue.' Only Simon had been treated for depression for a period with medication; a depression that was in part brought about by his move from Japan to Singapore.

Rages

For some of the teenagers, dealing with feelings of anger has been difficult at times. Rachel, for example, said, 'If there was one thing I could change about myself it would be my temper.' Similarly for Lee and his family, managing his anger and aggression had been a major issue during his childhood. Lee recalled how he was never able to observe the boundaries of acceptable behavior and that while other children would fight and know when to stop he would 'fight to the death.' His father said, 'The relationship with his peers broke down to the extent that they would enjoy winding him up to get the spectacular losses of temper.'

In many of the life stories, such as Lee's, anger seemed to be precipitated by the stresses of school, for example as a result of provocation by classmates, exhaustion at the end of a school day, or preschool nerves resulting in sudden explosions. For Sarah, moving to Singapore from Holland and starting a new school brought about regular angry outbursts, particularly towards her mother. Catherine, Sarah's mum, recalls: 'She would hold it in at school, but after school when she got to the car there would be screaming and abuse.' Sarah's uncontrollable rages and tantrums have lessened recently, and she has been taught strategies to try and manage them. One of the teenagers, Rachel, described how in the past she coped with feelings of anger and frustration by self-injuring, on some occasions quite seriously. Over time this response to feelings of anger has become less frequent and Rachel said, 'I don't bite or scratch myself as often as I used to – only when I'm really, really angry.'

Sometimes anger, even violence, can be seen as justified if the person believes that he or she had just cause. In some instances the AS teens' strong feelings of justification would override any consideration of the consequences of their actions. For example, although Rachel now concedes that it was wrong to hit a girl at school because that girl took her friend's pencil case, at the time she felt that the school's reaction – a week's detention and mention of 'assault' – was a huge over-reaction as she was entirely justified in correcting a wrong:

> At the time I felt that the school's reaction was really over the top because I didn't really see how defending a friend is so wrong. I was very upset that my mum and the head teacher were so disappointed in me. The head teacher actually called it an assault, which I still think is a little stupid, but I do see now that it was wrong for me to do what I did.

Lee also paid little thought to the consequences he would suffer from the school for his violent outbursts against the taunts of his classmates. This lack of reflection supports the theory that AS involves 'mindblindness' or an impaired sense of 'theory of mind' that prevents people with AS from considering how their actions might be viewed and judged by others (Baron-Cohen 1995). Those adolescents who did say that they could 'fly off the handle' also reported feeling more in control of themselves now than when they were younger, especially, as in Rachel's case, when they knew the danger signals of an impending outburst and had learned to control and channel their anger.

The blues

Feeling sad or depressed often arose from being on the outside of the social group or from being actively bullied, teased, or scorned by class-mates. Luke told us that he felt a lot happier during the weekend than during the school week. Lee remarked that he'd been happier since studying at Oxford as he felt that he could immerse himself in his study of mathematics and was finally surrounded by serious students.

However, some adolescents did comment that they sometimes felt overwhelmingly sad for no apparent reason, and that this feeling could last from a day, to a week, to, in Rachel's words, 'a couple of months.' Rachel wondered if she might 'one day need to take medication for depression.' Many of the parents we spoke to worried about depression, especially if the teenager spent an unusual amount of time at home or without friends, or seemed reluctant to leave the house even to join in family outings. Having a friend to talk to or being able to discuss your feelings to an understanding parent were seen as helpful in lifting the fog. Rachel said, '…eventually I'd go and talk to Mum about it and feel better than before.' The blues are worse when suffered alone.

The future

With the exception of Simon, the teenagers had definite career plans that they shared with us. In many instances the teens' special interests formed the basis for their career aspirations. With Lee and Luke, for example, their passion for information and communication technology resulted in their respective proposed career choices of computer programming and web design. Sarah was hoping to pursue a career that involved working with and looking after animals. Rachel expressed diverse interests, including graphic art, music, and Japanese, and was unsure which interest she would eventually pursue, although graphic or computer-aided design were strong possibilities. Chee Kiong's interest in the sciences had led him to select medicine as his intended profession.

The teenagers seemed confident about accomplishing their goals, although a few did express some anxieties about coping in a mainstream university. Rachel felt that she would need some sort of protected environment, a university with special education provision, or at the very least she would attend a tertiary institution close to home so she could continue living with her mother. Luke didn't find the idea of university appealing at all and was planning on obtaining his qualifications either through distance learning or a tertiary institution other than a university. Lee had already started at Oxford University when we met him and was living independently on campus. For Chee Kiong, the immediate worry after completing junior college was not university but coping with the mandatory two years in national service required of him in Singapore. His parents had petitioned the Ministry of Defense to place Chee Kiong in an administrative rather than a combat position.

Interestingly, all of the teens were positive that as they moved into adulthood Asperger Syndrome would be less significant in their lives. Already many of them had experienced a reduction in the behaviors, characteristics, and 'eccentricities' that had set them apart from their peers during childhood and led to the diagnosis. Lee in particular felt his AS traits had weakened to such an extent that, other than residual subtle difficulties in social understanding, Asperger Syndrome no longer defined him:

> In terms of self-definition, I wouldn't define myself as an 'Aspie' anymore, but I do see myself as a computer scientist. I feel there is a clear link between Asperger's and computer science. Look at Bill Gates — he's definitely got Asperger's, and I think that sort of sums up the connection. At present the only Asperger-related issue that exists is that I may do the odd socially inappropriate thing or make an inappropriate comment. Sometimes I feel people misinterpret my actions and comments, particularly some people may interpret my actions as personal attacks against them. Perhaps I don't always conduct things in the appropriate way and don't have a good grasp of all the complex social nuances of society.

Similarly, Rachel found it very difficult to identify which diagnostic criteria still described her. Her mother felt that at present the difficulties Rachel experienced were more to do with being a girl and a teenager rather than with AS.

Tony Attwood (1998) describes how moving into adulthood can be a relief for many individuals with Asperger's as they can leave behind some of the difficulties of adolescence, such as having to 'socialize with teenagers who can be cruelly intolerant, having different interests and objectives, coping with fluctuating emotions, and gaining insight into being different' (p.182). AS children often seem to have more affinity with adults than with other children (e.g. Chee Kiong's humorous quip 'I think primary school children really show their age, they are really childish'), so when at last they are adults, and no longer have to mix with children and teenagers, life may become easier (Attwood 1998). Chee Kiong, more so than any of the other teens, seemed to fit the AS stereotype of the 'miniature adult'; there was a sense that leaving behind the 'childishness of childhood' and the social travails of adolescence would be an immense relief for him. This feeling of relief at moving towards a time where each would have more control over their lives and more awareness of themselves and their strengths and weaknesses, was expressed in different ways by all the teens. While it would be an overstatement to say that the teens were experiencing a 'bad' adolescence, for most there was a feeling of optimism that things would only get better in the future.

Stephen Shore's description of journeying through the autism spectrum seems apt in describing the lives of the teens we spoke with. Most had progressed considerably along the spectrum through childhood and adolescence as a result of various factors: their own tenacity; their strengths and abilities; their ability to reflect on themselves and adapt; the support of their families; and the guidance of mentors along the way. It is difficult and unfitting to look at any child or adolescent and predict outcomes – who will be happy and successful and who will not – chance and circumstances as well as the individual's characteristics all play a role. And so it is the same with our group of teens. In hearing these stories, however, we were especially struck by the teenagers' resilience and enormous capacity for personal development. This bodes well for their futures.

Appendix A

The Narrative Approach in Research

Recently in disability studies, researchers have looked to new alternative methods of research that challenge the more traditional approach of the objective researcher (usually non-disabled) attempting to extract 'data' from the (disabled) research subject. One of these alternative methods is narrative research, which involves the study of texts to provide insight into personal and social experience (Clandinin and Connelly 1994; Goodley 2000). Narrative research involves the collection, writing up, and presentation of stories (Goodley 2000). Many writers have discussed the relationship between narrative – the telling of stories – and identity (e.g. Gergen and Gergen 1993; Shannon 1995; Somers 1994). In other words, we narrate stories about our experiences and our lives in order to understand more clearly who we are. Some advocates of the narrative approach further argue that the process is a reciprocal one, in which experience produces narrative and narrative in turn produces experience or is constitutive of our lives (Gergen and Gergen 1993). It has even been suggested that 'life is a story put into practice' (Gillman *et al.* 1997, p.680). Duplass and Smith (1995) describe the potentially transformative power of narrative in the life of a young teenager, Denis, who had been labeled severely emotionally disturbed. Through writing in the journal that he called 'The Novel of my Life and Thoughts,' Denis was able to create his own version or story of his life and in doing so redefine his identity:

> Once Denis had written his story, he could see clearly that he was suffering. His many pages exploring his life, his feelings about his mother, her feelings for him, and the anger he felt about how he was treated at home allowed him to see the puzzle and problems of his life more clearly. Once he became the author of his own story, he could change it. (Duplass and Smith 1995, p.147)

Narrative research encompasses many different methods such as biography, autobiography, life story, and life history. Goodley (2000) describes a life story as:

> the product of the reminiscences of one narrator that are structured together chronologically or thematically in a storied fashion. The life

story relies on the accounts of a primary narrator, whereas a life history combines different persons' stories of an individual. Life stories can be written alone or told to others who collaborate in writing. (p.48)

In this book we adopt a narrative approach to collaboratively create the life stories of six teenagers diagnosed with Asperger Syndrome. In addition, we also spoke to the parents of these teenagers to get their experiences and world views.

It is important here to differentiate between life histories/stories and case histories. Life histories provide a contrast to the 'tyranny of professional discourse' (Gillman *et al.* 1997) and the objectification of people with disabilities as presented in 'case histories.' Case histories are genres of medical discourse. A case history claims to present the objective truth about a patient or client – without any reference to what the patient is thinking or the thoughts or views of the person writing the report. The style of the case history also favors the reporting of behaviors or actions with little concern for the motives or feelings of the person being studied. Life histories and case histories also differ in how they are used. Case histories are primarily for the use of professionals to help categorize individuals and determine treatment. The lived experiences of the individual presented as the 'case' are usually invisible in these writings as if they have no stake in their own lives. In contrast, the aim of narrative approaches, such as life histories and life stories, is to convey the experience and world view of the narrator. Case histories often present a distorted view of events by focusing almost exclusively on the appropriateness or inappropriateness of an individual's behavior without any questioning of whether the social rule being violated or the context for the behavior is fair and just. Consider this example from a case study of a boy diagnosed with Asperger Syndrome:

January 1998 Incident

The committee met to discuss Michael's progress and the incidents that had resulted in Michael losing his temper and reacting violently in his regular classroom.

In one instance, an administrator came to the classroom to deliver donuts to students who had actively participated in singing the '12 Days of Christmas' at the school holiday party in January. The students had not been informed beforehand of any consequence for singing/not singing. Since Michael had not joined in the song, he did not receive a donut. He consequently threw a chair across the room.

The committee was concerned for now and for future behavioral episodes and wanted to help Michael learn to use immediate measures before he loses his temper. (Myles and Adreon 2001, p.185)

Obviously, Michael would benefit from learning new ways to cope with his anger. However, what's lacking in this narration is any account of Michael's thoughts and feelings. We have no sense of Michael's view of the situation. How did Michael interpret the dishing out of the donuts? The report also doesn't include any reflection on the practice of selectively awarding donuts to students. The only focus is on the inappropriateness of Michael's response and how it can be modified. The divorcing of Michael's behavior from the immediate social context and the exclusive focus on Michael's failure to keep his temper under control effectively maintain the status quo of the school's practices. The aim of the case history is not for us to get an 'insider' view of what it is like to be Michael. Rather it aims to present Michael from an 'outsider' viewpoint so as to confirm a diagnosis – in this instance Asperger Syndrome – and to provide strategies to help Michael adapt. From this brief example we can see that case histories and life histories greatly differ stylistically and in their aims and uses.

In his research on the self-advocacy movement of people with learning disabilities, Goodley (2000) presents a concise argument for the strengths and limitations of life stories. These strengths and limitations apply to our research on AS.

Strengths:

- *An invitation to personal stories:* Life stories represent the perspectives, attitudes, and perceptions of people with AS.

- *Addressing the abstract:* Life stories provide checks and balances to an overly theoretical, abstract, and over-deterministic view of AS, because they convey the particular experiences of individuals.

- *Story and meaning:* Life stories investigate some of the meanings held by narrators, and in this way they may cause readers to reevaluate their own preconceptions (e.g. that all people with AS are savants or are 'mindblind' or lack imagination or the ability to understand fictional narratives).

- *Exploring the research process:* Life stories involve a certain degree of reflection and evaluation of the research process on the part of the researcher. This reflection should provide a critical assessment of the ability of the research to authentically present the experience of others.

Limitations:

- *Only part of the story:* Life stories are limited in scope and provisional in the sense that people change their stories over time. Researchers may favor certain stories and repress the telling of others depending on their own research interests and agendas.

- *Bias in narrative:* All narrators make errors in the telling of their stories and all personal narratives are subject to bias. The information in life stories needs to be considered in light of accounts by other family members and factual information contained in official documents. (In the writing of this book, we endeavored to check the basic facts of each story with other family members and referred, when possible, to official documents, such as school and medical reports.)

- *Problems with relying on stories:* An overemphasis on stories may ignore other important social phenomena that the researcher needs to consider, such as economic or political factors affecting the narrator (e.g. economic depression or the restructuring of the provision of special education services within a particular country).

- *Problems with relying on storytellers:* Life stories require people to be able to clearly talk about their own experiences. A story is only as good as the storyteller. However, this means that the stories of people unable to talk about their lives in an engaging and articulate manner are never heard.

The Research Process

How we did the interviews

Our approach to interviewing was, as Taylor and Bogdan (1998) advise, 'to construct a situation that resembles those in which people naturally talk to each other about important things' (p.99). Interviews were relaxed and conversational, and exclusively conducted in the interviewee's home. An attempt was made to exchange information rather than just interrogate the interviewee by firing questions that needed to be answered. Anecdotes and incidents from our own experience of AS were offered when appropriate. First interviews were obviously more difficult, both for us and the interviewee, as we were 'getting to know each other' – though in one or two cases an almost instant rapport was established. In general we tried to keep the interviews as close as possible to everyday conversation, although obviously the flow of conversation was more one-sided. We attempted to be nonjudgmental, empathetic, and good listeners.

In all of our interviews we used an interview guide that listed the key topics of interest to us. The interview guide was not a structured questionnaire but rather a prompt to remind the interviewer of key topics that needed to be covered. During the interview the interviewer chose the order and phrasing of questions spontaneously. While we had key topics that needed to be covered, we also tried as much as possible to allow the interviewee to explore topics that he or she was interested in. We also primarily used open-ended and descriptive questions to get the interviewees to talk about the topics we were interested in without overtly structuring their responses (e.g. 'How would you describe yourself?' 'How would you describe a friend?' 'Tell me about your family. What sorts of things do you do together as a family?' 'Could you tell me about what your school day is like? What sorts of things do you do every day?' 'How would you describe Asperger Syndrome?'). Such questions allow the interviewer to explore a particular topic but also give the interviewee 'room to breathe' in terms of their responses. To add a further dimension to the life stories we also asked interviewees and their families if they would be willing to share with us any personal documents, such as letters, reports, records, and any relevant writings authored by them. We were very fortunate that all six families were so open and generous in sharing various personal documents with us. In Luke's case, his recently published book was a valuable resource. However, all of the teenagers we interviewed shared with us personal writings, letters, articles they had published, and other material.

We recorded each interview using a small micro-cassette recorder with a built-in condenser microphone, which we placed unobtrusively on a nearby table or chair. We then transcribed the interviews and sent the transcripts to the interviewees for their verification. We cross-checked the accuracy of factual information as well as some of the experiences outlined to us by the teenagers by also talking to the teens' parents to get their memories and perceptions of events and by consulting reports and other documents provided to us. After each interview we wrote up notes based on our impressions of the interview, personal observations, descriptions of the interview process, and any queries we wanted to follow up.

Writing the stories

Transforming transcripts into stories is not an easy task. There is always the risk that selecting certain words and anecdotes and excluding others changes the meaning of the information provided. The decisions the researcher makes in the process of shaping a narrator's spoken words into a written text have the potential to transform the information given, for better or worse. As Ferguson *et al.* (1992) point out, 'as soon as we, as researchers, become involved with helping other people tell their stories we inevitably become involved in telling *our* stories of *their* stories; we present our interpretations of their interpretations' (p.299).

In writing the stories, we tried, as much as possible, to keep to the words spoken during the interview although we occasionally used our own words to summarize anecdotes, correct grammar, and clarify meaning. This helped keep the narrative clear, concise, and flowing. For the sake of concision and readability we also omitted 'filler' language such as ums and 'you knows' and the like, as well as any repetitious information. The first drafts of the stories were then shown to narrators and, in this case, their parents. The families were urged to read the drafts carefully and provide feedback. Consequently, changes such as additions and deletions were made or negotiated. This interchange between narrator and writer ensured that the process was indeed collaborative and the final story, therefore, an authentic account of the narrator's views and experiences.

References

American Psychiatric Association (1994) *Diagnostic and Statistical Manual of Mental Disorders* (4th edition). Washington, DC: American Psychiatric Association.

Attwood, T. (1998) *Asperger's Syndrome.* London: Jessica Kingsley Publishers.

Attwood, T. (2000) 'The autism epidemic: Real or imagined?' http://www.tonyattwood.com.au/index.htm

Attwood, T. (2003) 'Cognitive behavior therapy.' In L.H. Willey (ed) *Asperger Syndrome in Adolescence.* London: Jessica Kingsley Publishers.

Baron-Cohen, S. (1995) *Mindblindness: An Essay on Autism and Theory of Mind.* Cambridge, MA: MIT Press.

Baron-Cohen, S. (2000) 'Is Asperger syndrome/high functioning autism necessarily a disability?' *Development and Psychopathology 12,* 489–500.

Baron-Cohen, S. (2003) *The Essential Difference: The Truth about the Male and Female Brain.* New York: Basic Books.

Blume, H. (1997) 'Autism and the internet or "It's the wiring, stupid".' *Media in Transition at M.I.T.* http://web.mit.edu/m-i-t/articles/blume.html

Clandinin, D.J. and Connelly, F.M. (1994) 'Personal experience methods.' In N. Denzin and Y. Lincoln (eds) *Handbook of Qualitative Research.* Thousand Oaks, CA: Sage.

Cockburn, L. (2002) 'Children and young people living in changing worlds: The process of assessing and understanding the "Third Culture Kid".' *School Psychology International 23,* 4, 475–485.

Duplass, D. and Smith, T. (1995) 'Hearing Denis through his own voice: A redefinition.' *Behavioral Disorders 20,* 2, 144–148.

Erikson, E. (1968) *Identity: Youth and Crisis.* New York: Norton.

Ferguson, P.M., Ferguson, D.L. and Taylor, S.J. (1992) 'Introduction.' In P.M. Ferguson, D.L. Ferguson and S.J. Taylor (eds) *Interpreting Disability: A Qualitative Reader.* New York: Teachers College Press.

Frith, U. (1991) *Autism and Asperger Syndrome.* Cambridge: Cambridge University Press.

Gergen, M.M. and Gergen, K.J. (1993) 'Narratives of the gendered body in popular autobiography.' In R. Josselson and A. Lieblich (eds) *The Narrative Study of Lives.* Thousand Oaks, CA: Sage.

Gillman, M., Heyman, B., and Swain, J. (2000) 'What's in a name? The implications of diagnosis for people with learning difficulties and their family carers.' *Disability and Society 15,* 389–409.

Gillman, M., Swain, J., and Heyman, B. (1997) 'Life history or "case" history: The objectification of people with learning difficulties through the tyranny of professional discourses.' *Disability and Society 12,* 675–693.

Gold, K. (2000) 'The high-flying obsessives.' *The Guardian,* December 12.

Goodley, D. (2000) *Self-advocacy in the Lives of People with Learning Difficulties.* Buckingham: Open University Press.

Goodley, D. (2001) 'Learning difficulties, the social model of disability and impairment: Challenging epistemologies.' *Disability and Society 16,* 207–231.

Gutstein, S.E. (2003) 'Can my baby learn to dance? Exploring the friendships of Asperger teens.' In L.H. Willey (ed) *Asperger Syndrome in Adolescence.* London: Jessica Kingsley Publishers.

Haddon, M. (2003) *The Curious Incident of the Dog in the Night-Time.* London: Jonathan Cape.

Howlin, R. (2003) 'Asperger syndrome in the adolescent years.' In L.H. Willey (ed) *Asperger Syndrome in Adolescence.* London: Jessica Kingsley Publishers.

Jackson, J. (2003) 'Families and parenting: The domino effect.' In L.H. Willey (ed) *Asperger Syndrome in Adolescence.* London: Jessica Kingsley Publishers.

Jackson, L. (2001) *A User Guide to the GF/CF Diet for Autism, Asperger Syndrome and AD/HD.* London: Jessica Kingsley Publishers.

Jackson, L. (2002) *Freaks, Geeks and Asperger Syndrome: A User Guide to Adolescence.* London: Jessica Kingsley Publishers.

Jackson, L. (2003, 7 August) 'Interview with *Ouch!*' http://www.bbc.co.uk/ouch/tvradio/autism/thoughts.shtml

Jackson, N. (2002) *Standing Down, Falling Up: Asperger's Syndrome from the Inside Out.* Bristol: Lucky Duck Publishing.

Molloy, H. and Vasil, L. (2002) 'The social construction of Asperger syndrome: The pathologising of difference?' *Disability and Society 17,* 659–669.

Moyes, R. (2003) 'Settling into the diagnosis of Asperger syndrome.' In L.H. Willey (ed) *Asperger Syndrome in Adolescence.* London: Jessica Kingsley Publishers.

Myles, B.S. and Adreon, M.A. (2001) *Asperger Syndrome and Adolescence: Practical Solutions for School Success.* Shawnee Mission, KS: Autism Asperger Publishing Company.

Oliver, M. (1990) *The Politics of Disablement.* London: Macmillan.

Polluck, D. and Van Reken, R. (1999) *Third Culture Kids: Growing up among Worlds.* Yarmouth, ME: Intercultural Press.

Sainsbury, C. (2000) *The Martian in the Playground: Understanding the Schoolchild with Asperger's Syndrome.* Bristol: Lucky Duck Publishing.

Shannon, P. (1995) *Text, Lies, and Videotape: Stories about Life, Literacy, and Learning.* Portsmouth, NH: Heinemann.

Shore, S. (2001) *Beyond the Wall: Personal Experiences with Autism and Asperger Syndrome.* Shawnee Mission, KS: Autism Asperger Publishing Company.

Shore, S. (2003) 'Disclosure for people on the autistic spectrum: Working towards better mutual understanding with others.' In L.H. Willey (ed) *Asperger Syndrome in Adolescence.* London: Jessica Kingsley Publishers.

Silberman, S. (2001) 'The geek syndrome.' *Wired,* December, 174–183.

Singer, J. (1999a) 'Human rights in education for "nerds", "weirdoes" and "oddballs" aka people on the autistic spectrum.' University of New South Wales, Sydney, Australia. Paper presented at the 1999 Conference on Human Rights, Education and Disability.

Singer, J. (1999b) '"Why can't you be normal for once in your life?" From "a problem with no name" to the emergence of a new category of difference.' In M. Corker and S. French (eds) *Disability Discourse*. Buckingham: Open University Press.

Somers, M. (1994) 'The narrative constitution of identity: A relational and network approach.' *Theory and Society 23*, 605–649.

Stanton, M. (2003) 'How do I be me?' In L.H. Willey (ed) *Asperger Syndrome in Adolescence*. London: Jessica Kingsley Publishers.

Taylor, S.J. and Bogdan, R. (1998) *Introduction to Qualitative Research Methods: A Guidebook and Resource*. New York: John Wiley and Sons.

Willey, L.H. (1999) *Pretending to be Normal*. London: Jessica Kingsley Publishers.

Willey, L.H. (2003) 'When the thunder roars.' In L.H. Willey (ed) *Asperger Syndrome in Adolescence*. London: Jessica Kingsley Publishers.

Wing, L. (1981) 'Asperger's syndrome: A clinical account.' *Psychological Medicine 11*, 115–129.

Subject Index

absolute thinking 130
    see also rigidity of thinking
ADD 100–2
ADHD 57–60, 61, 63, 72–3, 103–4, 147, 148
adulthood
    movement into 154–7
    see also career plans
affective disorders 152
    see also depression; tantrums
aggression 30–1, 33–4, 53–4, 152–4, 160–1
    see also bullying; tantrums
Asperger Syndrome
    characteristics 15–18, 21–2
    deficit approach 9–10, 18–22
    as a disability 9–10, 20–2, 40, 75–6, 118–21
    disclosure of 41, 49, 52, 63, 76–7, 109–10, 123–6, 138
    life stories *see* Chee Kiong; Lee; Luke; Rachel; Sarah; Simon
    in the media 14
    medical approach 9–10, 18–22, 160–1
    positive aspects 40, 52, 92, 119–20
    public perceptions 10–11, 117, 125, 126
    social constructionist approach 9–10
    see also absolute thinking; diagnosis; obsessions; savant abilities; social interaction; theory of mind; therapy
attention deficit hyperactivity disorder *see* ADHD
autism
    increase in diagnosis 14–15
    in siblings 46–7, 49, 53, 148

autistic spectrum 15
    progression along 17–18, 50, 92–3, 156

bias, in life stories 162
body language 16, 88
boredom 33
boyfriends *see* dating
brothers *see* siblings
bullying 140–1
    by young people with Asperger Syndrome 53–4
    Chee Kiong's experiences 73–4, 78, 79
    Lee's experiences 31, 33, 34, 38
    Luke's experiences 86–7, 97
    Sarah's experiences 67–8
    Simon's experiences 104, 106–7, 108–9
    see also marginalization; stigmatization

career plans 42, 56, 69, 83, 98, 154–5
case histories 160–1
cascin-free diet 89, 93
Chee Kiong 25
    at junior college 71, 76, 77–9, 80, 81–2
    at school 73–4, 80–1
    diagnosis 71, 75
    experience of bullying 73–4, 78, 79
    future plans 83
    hyperactivity 72–3
    language development 72
    military service concerns 71–2, 83
    response to Asperger Syndrome 74–7, 119, 125–6
    self-identity 74–7
    sensory issues 83
    social relationships 73–5, 77–80, 82
    tantrums 151
Chinnor Resource Unit 32, 35–6, 37–8
classroom discipline 30–1, 34, 36

Author Index

Attwood, T. 15, 17, 127, 133, 151, 152, 156

Baron-Cohen, S. 20–1, 120, 154
Blume, H. 120

Clandinin, D. J. and Connelly, F. M. 159
Cockburn, L. 145, 146

Duplass, D. and Smith, T. 159

Erikson, E. 122

Ferguson, P. M., Ferguson, D. L. and Taylor, S. J. 162
Frith, U. 15, 18

Gergen, M. M. and Gergen, K. J. 159
Gillman, M., Heyman, B. and Swain, J. 19, 20
Gillman, M., Swain, J. and Heyman, B. 159, 160
Gold, K. 14
Goodley, D. 10, 157–58, 159
Gutstein, S. E. 125, 127, 128, 129–30, 131, 133

Haddon, M. 14
Hall, K. 125
Howlin, R. 8, 115, 152

Jackson, J. 147, 149, 150
Jackson, L. 23, 85, 86, 88, 125, 127–8, 132
    see also Luke in subject index
Jackson, N. 7, 121, 125, 132

Molloy, H. and Vasil, L. 22
Moyes, R. 149

Myles, B. S. and Adreon, M. A. 160–1

Oliver, M. 9

Polluck, D. and Van Reken, R. 23

Sainsbury, C. 115, 125
Shannon, P. 159
Shore, S. 17–18, 117, 123, 156
Silberman, S. 14, 18
Singer, J. 20, 120
Somers, M. 159
Stanton, M. 147

Taylor, S. J. and Bogdan, R. 163

Willey, L. H. 9, 123, 131–2
Wing, L. 10, 15, 17